GLOBETROTTER™

Travel Guide

W9-CNL-039

IRELAND

ROBIN GAULDIE

NEW
HOLLAND

NEW
HOLLAND

★★★ Highly recommended
★★ Recommended
★ See if you can

Third edition published in 2008
by New Holland Publishers (UK) Ltd
London • Cape Town • Sydney • Auckland
10 9 8 7 6 5 4 3 2 1

website: www.newhollandpublishers.com

Garfield House, 86 Edgware Road
London W2 2EA, United Kingdom

80 McKenzie Street, Cape Town 8001
South Africa

Unit 1, 66 Gibbes Street, Chatswood,
NSW 2067, Australia

218 Lake Road, Northcote
Auckland, New Zealand

Distributed in the USA by
The Globe Pequot Press, Connecticut

This guidebook has been written by independent
authors and updaters. The information therein repre-
sents their impartial opinion, and neither they nor the
publishers accept payment in return for including in
the book or writing more favourable reviews of any
of the establishments. Whilst every effort has been
made to ensure that this guidebook is as accurate
and up to date as possible, please be aware that the
facts quoted are subject to change, particularly the
price of food, transport and accommodation. The
Publisher accepts no responsibility or liability for any
loss, injury or inconvenience incurred by readers or
travellers using this guide.

Keep us Current
Information in travel guides is apt to change, which
is why we regularly update our guides. We'd be
grateful to receive feedback if you've noted something we should include in our updates. If you have
new information, please share it with us by writing to
the Publishing Manager, Globetrotter, at the office
nearest to you (addresses on this page). The most significant contribution to each new edition will receive
a free copy of the updated guide.

Publishing Manager: Thea Grobbelaar
DTP Cartographic Manager: Genené Hart
Editors: Nicky Steenkamp, Thea Grobbelaar,
Mary Duncan, Donald Reid
Picture researchers: Shavonne Govender,
Carmen Watts
Design and DTP: Nicole Bannister, Éloïse Moss
Cartographers: Reneé Spocter, Genené Hart,
Nicole Bannister, Elaine Fick
Reproduction by Hirt & Carter (Pty) Ltd, Cape Town
Printed and bound by Times Offset (M) Sdn. Bhd.,
Malaysia.

Photographic credits:
Caroline Jones: pages 7, 27, 37, 45, 62, 80, 116;
Image Select: pages 13, 19, 20, 30; **Image
Select/Chris Fairclough:** title page, page 23; **Life
File/Fraser Ralston:** pages 25, 112, 113, 118, 119,
120; **Life File/Nigel Shuttleworth:** page 51; **Life
File/Robert Whistler:** page 115; **International
Photobank/Adrian Baker:** pages 9, 54, 58, 86, 90;
Ann Ronan Picture Library: page 18; **Peter Ryan:**
page 21; **Pictures Colour Library:** cover; **Neil
Setchfield:** pages 29, 34, 36, 42, 111; **Jeroen
Snijders:** pages 4, 6, 8, 10, 12, 14, 15, 16, 17, 24,
26, 28, 31, 32, 33, 38 [top and bottom], 39, 40, 41,
43, 44, 46, 47, 49, 50, 57, 64, 66, 67, 68, 69, 70,
71, 72, 74, 77, 78, 79, 81, 82, 83, 89, 91, 92, 94,
96, 98, 105; **Travel Ink/Trevor Creighton:** pages 60,
106; **Travel Ink/Abbie Enock:** pages 22, 102, 104;
Travel Ink/Ken Gibson: pages 59, 108; **Travel
Ink/Brian Mitchell:** page 100.

Cover: *The Castle of Ross was built in the 16th century.*
Title page: *Cliffs of Moher, County Clare.*

CONTENTS

1
Introducing Ireland

I reland is one of the world's most magical countries, with a history that stretches back into the mists of the **Celtic** twilight, landscapes that are by turns gently pastoral and ruggedly scenic, a culture whose wit and wisdom can equal those of any in the world, and a people whose reputation for a warm and lively welcome is for once matched by the reality.

Ireland's fascinating **history** – tragic, heroic and even, at times, quite comical – is well known, its myths carried by generations of emigrants to wherever the Irish have found a home.

But its present is equally fascinating. The Republic of Ireland is no longer one of Europe's poor relations. Instead, it is a dynamic **modern nation** whose breathtaking economic success in the 1990s has earned it the soubriquet 'Celtic Tiger', with the fastest economic growth in the European Union and also the youngest population. The Irish (if they ever were) are no longer a nation of potato farmers. They are instead a nation of electronic engineers, computer programmers, linguists and technocrats. But none of this progress has altered Ireland's essential, **irresistible charm**, nor its seductive effect on the visitor.

There's an old saying that there are two kinds of people in the world: those who are Irish and those who wish they were. After a visit (assuming you are not one of the lucky millions from all over the world who can count themselves Irish by descent) you may very well find yourself in the latter category.

TOP ATTRACTIONS

★★★ Dublin: cathedrals, Georgian buildings, Viking relics and the best nightlife in the home of Guinness.
★★★ Blarney Castle: home of the Blarney stone.
★★★ Cork City: Ireland's third city.
★★★ Belfast: balanced on the brink of peace, the gateway to the North.
★★★ Londonderry: historic, evocative city behind grim 17th-century ramparts.
★★★ Shannon-Erne Waterway: longest navigable river system in Europe.

Opposite: *Blarney Castle, the home of the famous Blarney Stone.*

THE LAND

Ireland's **location** on the extreme northwest fringe of Europe has had a profound effect through the ages on the island's geology, history and culture, as well as its flora and fauna.

Long before human habitation, two ice ages left their mark on the land, leaving ice-smoothed mountains and boulders, glacial valleys and hundreds of lakes.

Ireland's **remoteness** allowed a Celtic culture to flourish long after other Celtic nations in France and Britain had been absorbed by the Roman Empire. In addition, the island's early geological separation from mainland Europe created a unique range of flora and fauna.

The **Irish Sea**, separating Ireland from Britain, is only 18km (11 miles) wide at its narrowest point – the Northern Channel between Northern Ireland and the Scottish coast – and 192km (120 miles) at its widest – between Dublin and Liverpool – and reaches a maximum depth of 200m (656ft). The shallow waters of the **Continental Shelf**, around Ireland's Atlantic coast, plunge rapidly away into the depths of the Atlantic.

The island of Ireland is made up of a large **central lowland plain** of limestone, interrupted by low hills and partly hemmed in by a border of **coastal mountain ranges**. Ireland's geology is varied and distinctive: the southern mountains are old **red sandstone** (the oldest rock formation in the world) divided by **limestone** valleys. The mountains of Galway, Mayo and Donegal in the west and northwest, and those of Down and Wicklow on the east coast, are predominantly granite, and much of the northeastern region is covered by a **granite plateau**. The farmlands of the low-lying central plain are interrupted by large areas of ancient **peat bog** and many **lakes**.

Below: *Ireland's mountains were shaped by millennia of glaciation.*

Climate

Ireland, with a climate that gives it **mild wet winters** and **temperate wet summers**, thanks to the influence of the surrounding Atlantic Ocean and the Gulf Stream, can be visited year-round, though for touring, walking, or other outdoor activities, such as fishing, sailing or golf, the winter months – November to the end of March – are better avoided. Sub-zero temperatures and snow are quite rare, except on higher ground, and it is very unusual for summer **temperatures** to climb above 22°C (72°F),

Above: *A mild climate influenced by the Gulf Stream creates Ireland's green woodlands.*

even in the southern counties. **Rain** is always possible, even likely, at any time of year, and Ireland's weather is even more **changeable** than that of the neighbouring British Isles. In common with the rest of Europe, there are four very distinct **seasons**: spring (April–May), summer (June–September), autumn (October–November), and winter (December–March). July and August are the hottest months of the year, with temperatures reaching 14–16°C (57–61°F). January and February are the coldest, with mean daily temperatures of 4–7°C (39–45°F).

Although Ireland is quite a small island – only 486km (302 miles) from north to south and 275km (171 miles) from east to west at its longest and widest respectively – there is considerable local **variation** in weather. The exposed western coast, from Donegal in the north to Kerry in the south, receives somewhat greater rainfall and, in winter, occasional Atlantic gales, while the southern coasts of the Republic of Ireland have markedly softer winters than the windswept North Atlantic coast of Northern Ireland. **Rainfall** ranges from just 750mm (30 in) in some eastern areas to 1500mm (59 in) in the wettest western regions. In upland areas, rainfall can reach 2000mm (79 in) or more annually.

GEOGRAPHICAL STATISTICS

Total area: 84,421km² (32,595 sq miles).
Republic of Ireland: 70,282 km² (27,136 sq miles).
Northern Ireland: 14,139 km² (5459 sq miles).
Greatest length north to south: 486km (302 miles).
Greatest width east to west: 275km (171 miles).
Total coastline: 3,169km (1,970 miles).

IRELAND	J	F	M	A	M	J	J	A	S	O	N	D
MAX TEMP. °C	0	1	7	12	18	21	22	22	18	12	5	1
MIN TEMP. °C	-5	-4	-1	3	8	11	13	13	9	5	1	-3
MAX TEMP. °F	32	34	45	54	64	70	72	72	64	54	41	43
MIN TEMP. °F	23	25	30	37	46	52	55	55	48	41	34	27
HOURS OF SUN DAILY	2	2.5	5	6	8	8.5	9	8	6	4	2	1
RAINFALL mm	18	18	18	27	48	54	68	55	31	33	20	21
RAINFALL in	0.7	0.7	0.7	1.1	1.9	2.1	2.7	2.2	1.2	1.3	0.8	0.8
DAYS OF RAINFALL	13	11	10	11	13	12	13	12	10	13	12	13

Above: *Peat, excavated from ancient bogs, is an important fuel source.*

NATURAL RESOURCES

Lacking coal and oil and short of wood, turf (or **peat**) has been Ireland's staple fuel for centuries and still provides for up to 12 per cent of the nation's energy needs. **Bord na Mona** (the Peat Development Board) produces more than 4 million tonnes of peat annually. Ireland is also experimenting with **new energy sources** including solar power, hydro-electric power and wind power. Ireland's first **wind farm**, using giant windmills to drive electricity-generating turbines, opened at **Bella-corick** in Mayo in 1992.

Flora and Fauna

Ireland's geological separation from the European mainland followed the last Ice Age, resulting in a narrower variety of fauna and flora than in the rest of Europe.

Reptiles and **amphibians** are particularly scarce, with one species each of lizard, frog, newt and toad. The absence of snakes in Ireland, attributed to St Patrick, in fact long predates the arrival of Christianity.

That said, low population density across much of the island has allowed many indigenous species to flourish, with 135 breeding species of **bird**, and some 380 bird species recorded. Ireland's position on the edge of the Atlantic, relatively close to the Arctic Circle, attracts many migrant waterfowl species, especially in spring and autumn. Among them are some 75 per cent of the world population of the Greenland-dwelling white-fronted goose, which overwinter in Ireland.

As recently as 1000 years ago, most of the island was covered by primeval **deciduous forest** of oak, birch, holly, ash, yew, and hazel, and remnants of this ancient woodland survive in the Killarney area. Forestry programmes have led to the planting of extensive forests of spruce, pine and fir in many places. A dozen large state-run **forest parks**, and more than 400 smaller woodlands, are open to the public. In the Republic of Ireland, 75 **nature reserves** have been declared, including five dedicated to Irish fauna. In addition, there are five **national parks** managed by the Republic's National Parks and Wildlife Service, at Killarney, County Kerry; Glenveagh, County Donegal; Connemara, County Galway; the Burren, County Clare; and the Wicklow Mountains, County Wicklow.

Unique to Ireland are the **peat bogs** of the central plain, where centuries of bog-moss debris have gathered in deep layers wherever drainage is impeded. The unique **flora** of these areas includes many moss species, heathers and sedges, irises and orchids.

Also unique is **the Burren**, an expanse of barren carboniferous limestone in County Clare which shelters both Arctic-Alpine and Mediterranean plant species.

Ireland is a land of many **lakes** and **rivers**, with equally varied freshwater **fish** life, and some of the best trout and salmon fishing in the world. Other fish species include char, pollan and eel, and pike, perch, rainbow trout and roach have been introduced by anglers.

Mammal species number 31, all of them familiar to any visitor from temperate Europe or North America, though Irish subspecies of the common hare and the European stoat are unique to the island.

Offshore, particularly on Ireland's Atlantic coasts, visitors afloat may meet a range of **sea mammals** including grey seal, dolphin, porpoise, and several **whale** species, as well as large pelagic fish including **basking shark**. Loggerhead **turtles**, far off their usual feeding grounds in the Mediterranean and the Caribbean, occasionally fall foul of fishermen's nets.

BIRD-WATCHING

Ireland is great bird-watching country, with unique habitats that shelter many rare native and migrant species. On the 5631km (3500-mile) coast there are massive sea-bird colonies of **puffins**, **gannets**, **guillemots**, **gulls** and **terns**. Atlantic sea birds, including **auks**, **shearwaters** and **petrels**, migrate in huge numbers over the headlands of the west coast in spring and autumn, and inland the rivers and wetlands shelter myriads of ducks and waders such as **knot**, **golden plover**, **black-tailed godwit**, **brent** and **barnacle geese**, and thousands of **whooper swans**. Other species rare in the rest of Europe but present in numbers in Ireland include the **corncrake**, a summer migrant from North Africa, and the **red-billed chough**.

Left: *Seals are a common sight off Ireland's shores.*

Below: *Celtic crosses are frequently seen relics of Christianity in Ireland.*

HISTORY IN BRIEF

Very little is known of the first **Stone-Age** settlers in Ireland, who arrived as early as 7000BC, though peat bogs occasionally throw up ancient tools and ornaments. Some sites, such as the Neolithic tombs at **Newgrange**, have been excavated.

The first **metal users** arrived around 2000BC and many of their bronze tools and ornaments survive.

Though united culturally and linguistically, the island was divided among as many as 150 tiny kingdoms (*tuatha*) each ruled by a minor king owing allegiance to a more powerful ruler, who in turn was subject to one of five provincial kings (*ri ruich*). **War**, on a miniature scale, was almost constant. Social distinctions were rigid, from the tuath and his warriors down to workers and slaves. The **economy** was based on barter, with the cow as the basic exchange unit. Elaborate gold brooches and arm rings testify to the metalworking skills of the Celtic smiths.

Ireland escaped **Roman** conquest, and this golden age of the Celts lasted many centuries longer than elsewhere. In the 5th century AD, the outside world made its first major impact for more than a thousand years, with the arrival of Christian missionaries. Just as Roman-British civilization was being snuffed out, **Christianity** found a new toe-hold in Ireland, with the founding of great monasteries.

Christianity was able to flourish unmolested by the barbarian invaders who destroyed the Western Roman Empire, and Ireland became an outpost of Christian culture. The **monasteries** became the centres of learning and culture. From the 6th century onward, Irish missionaries were to bring Christianity back to the British Isles.

HISTORICAL CALENDAR

ca 7000BC First Stone-Age people settle in Ireland.
500BC or later First iron-using Celts settle in Ireland.
ca AD432 St Patrick begins conversion to Christianity.
8th–9th century Viking raids followed by settlements.
10–11th century Era of Irish dynastic wars. Boru gradually gathers Ireland under his rule.
1014 Battle of Clontarf. Boru's army victorious, Boru killed.
1169–70 Norman invasion of Ireland led by Richard FitzGilbert de Clare, Earl of Pembroke, nicknamed Strongbow (1130–76).
1170 Richard FitzGilbert de Clare captures Dublin.
1171 Henry II of England claims Ireland.
15th century English territory reduced to 'the Pale' – counties of Dublin, Kildare, Louth and Meath – as a result of the War of the Roses.
1536 Revolt of Earl of Kildare put down, Kildare executed.
1580–83 Revolt against Crown in Munster and Leinster.
1595–1601 Revolt of O'Neill of Ulster with Spanish support.
Early 17th century King James VI & I encourages 'Plantation' of Scottish Presbyterian settlers in Ulster.
1641–52 Ireland drawn into England's Civil War. Massacres at Drogheda and Wexford by Cromwell's troops.
1688–91 'War of the Two Kings'; Catholic supporters of deposed James II against Protestant William III (of Orange).
1800 Act of Union makes Ireland part of UK.
1803 Emmet's rebellion.

1829 Legislation to permit Catholics to sit in Parliament.
1845 Beginning of the great potato famine.
1848 'Young Ireland' revolt is defeated.
1858 Formation of Irish Republican Brotherhood.
1859 Foundation of Fenian Brotherhood by exiles in USA.
1867 Fenian uprising crushed.
1873 Foundation of Home Rule League.
1882 Assassination of Lord Cavendish in Phoenix Park.
1890–1916 Pressure for Irish independence increases.
1905 Formation of nationalist Sinn Fein in Dublin and of Protestant Ulster Volunteer Force in the north.
1912 Third Irish Home Rule Bill is introduced.
1913 The Irish Citizens' Army is formed.
1914 Outbreak of World War I. British government withdraws Home Rule Bill.
1916 Easter Rising in Dublin.
1918 Sinn Fein election victory; Dail Eireann (the Irish Parliament) is formed.
1921 Anglo-Irish Treaty agrees limited self-rule.
1922 Foundation of Irish Free State. Civil War breaks out between hardline independence fighters and 'Free Staters'.
1949 Ireland becomes a republic and withdraws from British Commonwealth.
1968 'Civil Rights' marches in Northern Ireland broken up.
1969 British troops arrive in Northern Ireland. Provisional IRA escalates violence.
1970s IRA bombing continues in UK and Northern Ireland.

1971 Internment without trial introduced for suspected terrorists in Northern Ireland.
1972 'Bloody Sunday' and 'Bloody Friday'. Stormont Parliament suspended.
1972 Unionist strikes and protests destroy Sunningdale 'power-sharing' agreement. Direct rule from Westminster.
1973 Ireland joins European Economic Community.
1981 Bobby Sands elected Sinn Fein's first MP. Sands and eight others die on hunger strike. Sinn Fein's 'ballot box and Armalite' strategy.
1984 IRA attempt to assassinate Margaret Thatcher.
1990 Mary Robinson is Ireland's first woman president.
1996 Secret meetings between British Government and Sinn Fein leaders.
1997 IRA and Protestant paramilitary groups announce ceasefires.
1998 Good Friday multiparty talks; agreement to form Northern Ireland Assembly.
1998 Referendum in May; David Trimble elected First Minister of the Assembly.
1998 'Real IRA' kills 11 in Omagh bombing in September. Outrage forces hardliners to declare ceasefire.
1998 David Trimble and John Hume receive Nobel Peace Prize.
2005 The IRA agree to disarm voluntarily.
2007 The Reverend Ian Paisley of the Democratic Unionist Party and Gerry Adams of Sinn Fein agree to a devolved parliament in Northern Ireland.

Above: *The National Museum in Dublin is a treasury of Irish history.*

The Vikings

The second wave of outsiders were less welcome, if equally influential in the long run. The first Viking longships appeared in AD795, and for the next 40 years Viking **raiders** struck again and again, plundering monasteries for their treasures and farmlands for their cattle. It was at this time that Ireland's characteristic round towers were built. They served as lookout posts and refuges from the raiders, and today some still stand as proud examples of Ireland's earliest architecture. Most raiders came at first from **Norway**, though later raiders came from Viking colonies in **Orkney**, **Iceland** and the **Hebrides**. By the 9th century Viking fleets were appearing in great strength, with up to 60 ships and more than 3000 men. **Dublin Bay**, a natural harbour on the Irish Sea, was an ideal base for them. In AD841–842 Vikings began to establish permanent year-round settlements at promising anchorages around the coast, including Dublin, Waterford, Cork and Limerick. From the 10th century onward the **Norse kings** were a permanent fixture on the Irish scene, fighting amongst themselves and in alliance with native Irish rulers.

They were traders as well as raiders, and their **commerce** with ports in the Baltic, the North Sea and the Mediterranean made Dublin, for almost three centuries, one of western Europe's wealthiest seaports and ended Ireland's splendid isolation once and for all. At **Wood Quay** in Dublin, where the walls and layout of the original Norse city were discovered during building works, archaeologists have found 10th-century gold and silver coins and glassware from **Scandinavia**. Later finds indicate that by the 12th century there was trade with **England** and **Normandy**.

Brian Boru

The Vikings were helped by constant wars between Irish petty kings. Brian Boru, the great Irish warrior king, was the first leader to come close to ruling the entire island. By the second half of the 10th century Boru was King of North Munster, and after 25 years of almost continual warfare he proclaimed himself **High King of Tara**, traditional seat of the most powerful of all the kings of Ireland. In 997 he took Dublin, defeating a revolt by the Dublin Vikings in 999. In 1013 his greatest rival, **Mael Morda**, king of Leinster, rose against him, bringing in a huge Viking army. They met at **Clontarf**, on Good Friday 1014. Irish and Viking chroniclers record that the battle was fierce even by the standards of those bloody times. Though Boru's army won the day, slaying both Mael Morda and the Viking Earl Sigurd of Norway, both Boru and his son and heir **Murchadh** also fell. The battle is often claimed as an Irish victory which ended the threat of Viking conquest, though in fact the Viking star was no

---

ILLUMINATED MANUSCRIPTS

The **monasteries** of Ireland produced illuminated manuscripts withglowing, Celtic-influenced patterns and characters. These were sought after as **objects of prestige** by kings and noblemen. Students came from overseas to study under Irish masters in the scriptoria of the great monasteries, where texts like the famous *Book of Kells* were produced.

Below: *The Book of Kells is the best preserved example of an early Irish illuminated manuscript.*

MEDIEVAL ARCHITECTURE

Apart from standing stones, and the passage tombs such as those at **Newgrange**, Ireland has few buildings more than 1000 years old. Among the oldest surviving buildings are **stone beehive huts** built by monks or hermits on remote islands, and typically Irish **round towers**, also built by monks as refuge against Viking raiders in the 10th to 12th centuries. Small **Romanesque churches** and **chapels** began to be built in the 12th century, and the Norman invaders built large **cathedrals** in the Gothic style. The Normans also built **castles**, first in wood, then in stone, and by the early 15th century the nobles and clan chiefs were building **fortified tower houses**, many of which survive.

longer ascendant, and Vikings fought (as usual) on both sides. Long after Clontarf, Dublin was ruled by Vikings, one of whom, **Sitric Silkenbeard**, built the first cathedral, Christ Church, in 1038. It was replaced by a stone cathedral in 1172. No successor was strong enough to replace Boru as High King, and the island once again became a mosaic of squabbling mini-kingdoms.

The Normans

By the mid-12th century, the Norman conquerors of England had acquired Irish ambitions. In 1170 a Norman force led by the Earl of Pembroke, **Richard FitzGilbert de Clare** (1130–76), nicknamed 'Strongbow', took Dublin. In 1172 **King Henry II** took Dublin under royal protection and in 1177 proclaimed his son John (later King John II of England) Lord of Ireland.

In the vast areas of Ireland which were covered with bog and thick forest, the Norman warhorses and chain-mail were useless. **Beyond the Pale** – an earth rampart thrown up to protect Dublin and the surrounding counties – the Irish kings ruled unchallenged. The Anglo-Norman conquerors were influenced by their Irish subjects, adopted the Irish tongue, married into Irish noble families, and gradually became more Irish than English. In 1316 Ireland was drawn into the war between

England and Scotland when **Edward Bruce**, brother of the Scottish King Robert, invaded Ireland. Bruce came close to taking Dublin before being killed, at **Faughart**, in 1318. The **Wars of the Roses**, between the English noble houses of Lancaster and York, left the Anglo-Irish earls free to rule as they chose, and the **Fitzgerald** family of Kildare emerged as the most potent of them.

From the 16th to the 18th Century

By the 16th century the Anglo-Irish had become almost independent of the English crown. When England converted to **Protestantism** under **Henry VIII**, Anglo-Irish nobles and the Irish people remained staunchly Catholic, and religion became an issue. In 1541 Henry VIII declared himself **King of Ireland** – earlier kings

had used the title Lord of Ireland – and decreed that all Irish lands were crown property. When Catholic Spain set out to crush heretic England in the reign of **Elizabeth I**, it found allies in Ireland. The country was ravaged by repeated rebellions.

The greatest **rising** of the era was led by **Hugh O'Neill**, Earl of Tyrone (1540–1616). At first a protégé of the English, he turned against the crown in 1598 and defeated an English army at the **Yellow Ford**, putting Ireland almost in his grasp. In 1601 the arrival of a **Spanish** force at **Kinsale**, in County Cork, made England's position even more precarious but, after a decisive defeat at Kinsale, O'Neill surrendered. He was eventually pardoned, and fled to France in 1607.

Under Elizabeth I, England began the first campaigns to conquer Ireland thoroughly and completely by destroying the traditional Irish way of life, which the English had come to see as barbaric. Chieftains were to be deposed, ordinary people were to be dispossessed to make way for **Loyalist Protestant settlers** from England and Scotland, and increasingly the Protestant religion was to be imposed. One of the solutions adopted by the English was to offer **land grants** to Protestant English and Scots settlers, giving them farmland confiscated from the Irish.

Above: *James Fort, situated at Kinsale, was built in order to defend a natural harbour from French and Spanish invaders.*

Opposite: *The passage tombs at Newgrange are among Ireland's few truly ancient buildings.*

HIGH KINGS

Throughout the first millennium AD, scores of petty kingdoms fought among themselves and paid lip service to a high king, or *Árd Rí*, who might rule as much as a quarter of the island, which was traditionally divided into four large regions – **Ulster**, **Leinster**, **Munster** and **Connaught**. The ceremonial seat of the High King, at **Tara**, is still marked by a ring of ancient **standing stones**.

Right: *Effigy of King William III, Protestant victor of the Battle of the River Boyne, at King John's Castle.*

Opposite: *Monument to Wolfe Tone, leader of the United Irishmen, commemorates the abortive rising of 1798.*

THE WILD GEESE

As the English tightened their grip on Ireland, many Irish chiefs and their followers left for **Europe**, entering the service of the Catholic rulers of Austria, Spain and France. With the defeat of James II in 1690, this exodus reached its peak and thousands of Irishmen served as **soldiers of fortune** in continental armies under Irish generals like Mac-Mahon, Taaffe, O'Neil and Butler. Others served even further afield: the St Patrick's Battalion of Irish soldiers served in the Mexican army fighting the **United States** in 1847. Irishmen also served with distinction in the British Army during **World War II**. Since independence, Ireland has been strictly neutral, but members of its Defence Forces have served with excellence all over the world in the blue berets of the **United Nations** peace-keeping forces.

In 1641, there was another great rising, and in 1642 Ireland was drawn into the **English Civil Wars** with Irish Catholics backing King Charles and Protestant settlers the Parliamentarian side. In 1649 the troops of **Oliver Cromwell**, Lord Protector of England, finally crushed Irish Royalist resistance.

The Cromwellian regime was followed by the return of the Stuart dynasty to the throne in the person of **Charles II**, but strong anti-Catholic feeling in England brought little hope for Ireland.

Catholic hopes were raised when **James II**, brother of Charles II, came to the throne in 1685. James, a Catholic, intended to restore the Roman Church in England and Ireland. In 1688, however, the English parliament toppled James and invited the Dutch prince **William of Orange**, who was married to James's daughter Mary, to take the throne. James fled to Ireland to seek Catholic support, plunging the country once more into turmoil. In 1690, however, his army was defeated in battle at the **River Boyne**, and William completed his triumph in 1691 gaining for the Protestant minority in Ireland an ascendancy that would last throughout the 18th century and well into the 19th.

The **Dublin Parliament**, with a permanent Protestant majority, banished Catholic clergy and debarred Catholics from teaching, marrying Protestants, or taking court action in land cases. Throughout Ireland, Catholics were dispossessed of their land. In 1641, 59 per cent of Irish land was Catholic-owned. By 1714, only seven per cent was in Catholic hands, and that mostly in the poorest and remotest parts of the country.

The Protestant Irish elite known as the **Ascendancy** dominated the country and also the Irish parliament throughout the 18th century, maintaining a gracious way of life at the expense of their Irish tenantry. The high point of their power came in 1782, when their demands for the right to pass **separate laws** for Ireland grew louder and were granted.

The French Revolution encouraged a group led by the Dublin-born Protestant **Wolfe Tone** (1763–98) to form the **United Irishmen**, whose aim was to unite Protestant and Catholic communities in a campaign for parliamentary reform. Banned in 1796, the United Irishmen became a revolutionary movement aligned with Republican France, where Tone fled to seek support for an **independent Irish republic**. In December 1796, Tone arrived at **Bantry Bay** with a French force of 36 ships and 15,000 men. But everything went awry. A strong east wind prevented the invaders from landing, giving the authorities time to hunt down Tone's supporters in Ireland. Tone's rebellion, when it finally came in 1798, was a pathetic affair, backed by only 1000 French troops. Landing in Mayo in August 1798, they first routed a militia force at **Castlebar**, but were soon defeated by vastly stronger British forces.

IRISH MEXICANS

The 100 Irishmen of the **San Patricio Regiment** who fought for Mexico in its war with the United States (1846–48) may have been, as the Americans claim, deserters from the US Army, but **John Riley**, from Galway, the regiment's commander, his second in command, Mayo-born **Patrick Dalton**, and their men are heroes to Mexicans. In 1999, the Irish president, **Mary McAleese**, laid a wreath on their **monument** in Mexico City while on a **State visit to Mexico** and was presented with the keys to the city.

The Act of Union

In 1800 the British government dismantled the Irish parliament and initiated direct rule from London, **uniting** the two kingdoms of **England and Ireland** by the Act of Union which took effect from 1801. Throughout the century, peaceful agitation for the return of Irish affairs to the control of an Irish Parliament was paralleled by rural violence. In 1803, the republican **Robert Emmett** (1778–1803) led 90 men (Emmett had hoped for 2000) to attack **Dublin Castle**. They were quickly rounded up and transported or hanged. The greatest advocate of peaceful means was **Daniel O'Connell** (1775–1847) who campaigned for an independent Irish parliament which would reflect the Catholic majority in Ireland but remain subject to the British Crown. O'Connell's mass rallies made him a formidable figure, and his election to Parliament in 1828 forced the British government to allow Catholics to become Members of Parliament. O'Connell continued to campaign for the repeal of the Act of Union. In 1846, charged with conspiracy, he was briefly imprisoned, then left for Italy, where he died in 1847.

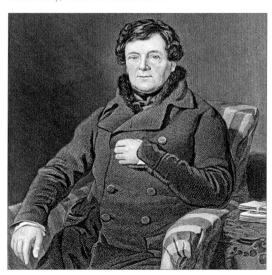

Opposite: *Hundreds of thousands of Irish people starved to death in the great potato famine of the 1840s.*

Right: *Daniel O'Connell, the great 19th-century Irish patriot and Home Rule campaigner.*

The Famine

The most significant and symbolic event of the first half of the 19th century was the great potato famine which struck Ireland between 1845 and 1849. By the 1840s, Ireland's peasantry depended completely on the potato. In many parts of the country they ate little

else. When the **potato blight** struck, the result was famine, made worse by the British government's reluctance or inability to provide alternative food supplies. Hundreds of thousands **starved**, and many more **emigrated** during the famine and in the years that followed. In 1841 Ireland had a population of around eight million. Today, its population is half that, while tens of millions of Americans, Australians, Canadians, New Zealanders and others claim Irish descent.

Irish nationalism drew strength from the bitter anger which followed. In 1858 **James Stevens** launched the **Fenian** movement, and renewed Fenian risings punctuated the second half of the 19th century.

The constitutional nationalists were led for most of this time by **Charles Stuart Parnell**, a Protestant and the Member of Parliament for West Meath, whose campaigning for fairer rents and land tenure for the Irish peasant won him widespread support. In 1881 Parnell's demands for **Irish Home Rule** led to his being jailed in Kilmainham Gaol in Dublin. He was, however, released in 1882 on condition that he work against violence, but the murder of **Lord Frederick Cavendish**, British chief secretary for Ireland, by the **Invincibles**, an extremist group, wrecked the somewhat shaky alliance between Parnell and the British government of **William Ewart Gladstone's** Liberal Party.

THE GREAT HUNGER

The greatest tragedy in Ireland's history began in 1845, when a severe **blight** caused by the fungus *Phytophthora infestans* struck the **potato crop**. The potato, introduced from the Americas in the 17th century, had quickly become the **staple food** of the Irish peasantry. Between 1800 and 1840 the population had almost doubled, with most living perilously close to the hunger line. The blight turned potatoes into inedible black slime; 800,000 **starved** to death, and hundreds of thousands more were forced to **emigrate**. Thousands died in the so-called '**coffin ships**' taking them to America. The famine, which lasted for four years, was made worse by the British government's initial **refusal to interfere** with the workings of the free market by distributing cheap grain or bread. Not until 1847 did the government pass legislation to help feed the starving.

Right: *The Four Courts in Dublin burns during the Civil War of 1922–23.*
Opposite: *A statue of Countess Markievicz, the first woman elected to the British Parliament, resting at St Stephen's Green.*

Gladstone introduced the first Irish Home Rule Bill in 1886, but was defeated. In 1890 **scandal** surrounded Parnell because of his affair with a married woman. He was ousted from the leadership of his movement and died the following year.

Self-government seemed no closer than before. In 1905 **Arthur Griffith** launched **Sinn Fein**, a party calling for an independent Irish Parliament in Dublin. Meanwhile, **James Connolly**, soon to be a leading light in the nationalist movement, was cutting his revolutionary teeth as an organizer of Dublin's new trade union movement. Constitutional reform received new impetus when the Irish Nationalists at Westminster briefly held the balance of power in 1912. In Northern Ireland, anti-nationalist Protestants formed the **Ulster Volunteer Force** and began arming themselves. In the south, nationalists formed the **Irish Volunteers**. Ireland seemed poised for civil war when in 1914 the outbreak of **World War I** temporarily united Protestant loyalists and moderate nationalists behind Britain.

The Easter Rising
Militant republicans had other ideas. On Easter Monday 1916 the **Irish Republican Brotherhood**, forerunners of the Irish Republican Army, attacked British forces in Dublin. Barricaded into the **Dublin Post Office**, the tiny force hoped in vain for a mass rebellion.

The British bombardment of the post office and other rebel positions in central Dublin over the next six days caused heavy civilian casualties. When the rebels surrendered, they had lost 64 men and had killed 130 British soldiers, while 300 civilians also died.

The execution of 15 ringleaders made them martyrs to the cause of freedom. The nationalist movement was soon dominated by republican militants. **Sinn Fein** won 73 seats in the 1918 general election, the **Irish Nationalists** won six and the **Ulster Unionist Party** took 16, all in the north. Sinn Fein refused to take up its seats at Westminster, instead setting up the **Dail Eireann** (Irish Assembly) with **Eamon de Valera** as President. The scene was set for partition.

War and Civil War

The Irish Republican Army fought the British Army and the Royal Irish Constabulary from 1919 to 1921, finally forcing Britain to concede self-rule to the 32 counties which now form the **Republic of Ireland**. The six northern, Protestant-majority counties of Londonderry, Antrim, Down, Armagh, Tyrone and Fermanagh remained **part of the United Kingdom**.

Within the new Irish Free State, fighting began between the hardline Republican movement, led by de Valera, which refused to recognize the treaty, and the new government. In 1923, de Valera agreed to surrender.

The Irish Free State retained constitutional ties with Britain until 1949, when it severed all links to become a republic. In 1973 Ireland joined the European Union.

COUNTESS MARKIEVICZ

Constance Georgine, Countess Markievicz (1868–1927), nee Constance Gore-Booth, married a Ukrainian nobleman who deserted her in Dublin in 1913. In 1908 she **joined Sinn Fein** and in 1916 took part in the **Easter Rising**, commanding volunteers in action against the British. Sentenced to death, she was reprieved and went on to become the **first woman** elected to the **British Parliament** – as Sinn Fein member for Dublin St Patrick's – and after independence was a member of the Dail until her death.

CONSTANCE MARKIEVICZ

MAJOR
IRISH CITIZEN ARMY
1916

EAMON DE VALERA

Eamon de Valera (1882–1975) joined the **Irish Volunteers** in 1913 and was sentenced to death as a ringleader of the **Easter Rising**. Reprieved in 1917, he became president of the republican movement **Sinn Fein**, and was arrested again in 1919. He escaped to the USA, returning in 1920 to lead **IRA opposition** to the treaty which divided Ireland. Following the Civil War he led the **Fianna Fail** party in and out of government for a generation, and became president of the Republic of Ireland in 1959.

Northern Ireland since Independence

The North had not only a **Protestant** ruling class but a fiercely Presbyterian and Unionist working-class majority. After the creation of the Irish Free State, the Unionists created in **Ulster** a Protestant fortress which, through legal and covert discrimination, effectively prohibited Catholics from power. A paramilitary police force, the notorious **B Specials**, was exclusively Protestant. In the late 1960s protest marches led by the **Catholic Civil Rights Movement** were violently broken up by the B Specials, and Catholic districts were attacked by Protestant mobs. The violence played into the hands of the **IRA**, which had never given up hope of making the 'Six Counties' part of the Republic. When British troops were sent in 1969, they were initially welcomed, but soon became targets for IRA snipers.

A split between the Dublin-based, left-leaning 'Official' IRA and more traditionally-minded Catholic nationalists in the North led to the creation of the **Provisional IRA**, which quickly came to dominate the armed struggle and initiated the bombing of 'economic targets' (ranging from pubs to government offices) as well as attacks on Army and Royal Ulster Constabulary patrols and bases. By 1972, the annual death toll had reached 467, with more than 10,000 non-fatal shootings

Below: *Catholic protesters march in Northern Ireland under the eyes of the security forces.*

and more than 1800 bombings. There were 21,000 British troops on the streets of Northern Ireland. Internment without trial of terrorist suspects created a climate in which the IRA, and Unionist terror groups, flourished. The shooting of 13 civilians during a demonstration in Londonderry's fiercely Catholic **Bogside** district on '**Bloody Sunday**' (30 January 1972) was the most notorious of many incidents in which civilians were killed by army bullets. On '**Bloody Friday**', in July 1972, the IRA exploded 22 bombs in **Belfast**, killing nine. The suspension of the **Northern Ireland parliament** in March 1972 and the introduction of direct rule from London (with Northern Ireland MPs sitting in the British House of Commons) did nothing to allay the violence, which spread to the British mainland with IRA bombs in London and other cities. In the last shaky years of **James Callaghan's** Labour government, a handful of hardline Ulster Unionist MPs, most notably **Dr Ian Paisley**, held the balance of power in the British Parliament, giving them disproportionate influence. In 1979, the election of arch-Conservative **Margaret Thatcher** as Prime Minister made any possibility of negotiation with the nationalists even more remote.

Above: *Belfast graffiti supports the Loyalist paramilitary Ulster Volunteer Force.*

WHAT'S IN A NAME?

Article 4 of the **Irish Constitution** provides that the name of the state is **Eire**, or in English the **Republic of Ireland**. Normal practice is to use Eire only in Irish texts and to use Ireland in English-language documents. **Nationalists**, reluctant to confer any legitimacy on the partition of the island, sometimes refer to the Republic as 'the 26 counties' and to Northern Ireland as 'the six counties'. **Unionists** frequently refer to the North simply as 'Ulster'.

In 1981 the election of an imprisoned IRA volunteer, **Bobby Sands**, to the parliamentary seat of Fermanagh and South Tyrone ushered in what became known as the 'Armalite and ballot box' policy. Sands died on hunger strike and became an instant martyr. In 1982, **Gerry Adams**, leader of Sinn Fein, the political party aligned with the IRA, was elected to Parliament. This move signalled no cessation of the armed struggle; on 15 September 1984 the IRA attempted to blow up the entire British Cabinet during the Conservative Party's annual conference in **Brighton**. Five people were killed but the politicians escaped with their lives. In 1986 nationalists agreed to end their opposition to seeking election to the Dail (which dated from the Civil War), and Sinn Fein campaigned for election to seats in the Republic (nationalist MPs Gerry Adams and Martin McGuinness never took up their seats at Westminster). In 1987 the death of 11 people in the bombing of a **Remembrance Day** service at **Enniskillen** marked a turning point, with even Gerry Adams declaring it 'a terrible mistake' while refusing to condemn the use of violence. By 1988, 2705 had died in the Troubles, more than 60 per cent of them at the hands of the Provisional IRA and nationalist splinter groups such as the **Irish National Liberation Army**. (In the 1990s further killings were carried out by Loyalist terror groups.)

WHO'S WHO?

Fianna Fail, founded in 1926, and **Fine Gael**, founded in 1933, have dominated Irish politics since independence. Fianna Fail is more conservative on many issues, but the parties are not clearly divided along conventional left-right lines. Left of both stands the **Labour Party**, which has sometimes allied with Fine Gael in coalitions. Other parties represented in the Dail include the **Progressive Democrats**, a modernizing liberal party with a pro-EU agenda; the **Democratic Left**, a soft-left 'third way' party; and the **Green Party**, which won its first seat in 1989.

Towards a Settlement

From 1990, tentative diplomacy between the government of Margaret Thatcher's successor, **John Major**, the moderate Nationalist Social Democratic Labour Party, and Sinn Fein and the IRA, seemed to offer the best chance yet of peace. On 1 September 1994 the IRA announced 'complete cessation of military operations' but when talks failed IRA bombs exploded in Manchester and London.

The election of **Tony Blair's** Labour Government in May 1997, and the intervention of US President Bill Clinton, paved the way for new talks and after lengthy negotiations the IRA, followed by other terrorist organizations on both sides, agreed to a permanent cease-fire. The **Good Friday Agreement** of 1998 provided for the setting up of a Northern Ireland Assembly, ratified by referendum in the Republic and the North, and elections were held shortly after, with the election of **David Trimble**, leader of the mainstream Ulster Unionists, as First Minister and **Seamus Mallon**, deputy leader of the Social Democratic Labour Party, as his deputy. Sinn Fein took a substantial proportion of the vote and several seats, but its participation in the First Assembly's executive remained problematic. In 2007 the Reverend Ian Paisley of the Democratic Unionist Party and Gerry Adams of Sinn Fein agreed to a devolved parliament in Northern Ireland.

THE IRISH ABROAD

Descendants of Irish emigrants have played a leading role in the history of many nations. In the **USA**, where some 40 million claim Irish ancestry, at least three presidents this century alone – **John F Kennedy**, **Richard M Nixon** and **Ronald Reagan** – have been of Irish stock. In **Australia**, up to 30 per cent of the population is estimated to be of Irish descent, as are 15 per cent of **New Zealanders**. Irish emigrants also settled in **South America**, where Mayo-born **William Brown** founded the Argentinian Navy and **Bernardo O'Higgins** became the first president of Chile.

Opposite: *Bobby Sands, the IRA volunteer who died on hunger strike, was one of a long line of Republican martyr figures.*
Left: *Nationalist graffiti on the strongly Catholic Falls Road demands the disbandment of the Royal Ulster Constabulary.*

MORE JOBS

Unemployment in the Republic of Ireland hit a 16-year low in early 1999 when it dropped to 6.7 per cent, well below the European Union average of 9.8 per cent. Unemployment dropped steadily from early 1997 onward, inevitably leading the government to claim credit for a **strong economy** translating growth into jobs. One factor has been the huge growth of the **information technology industry**, with government initiatives to retrain unemployed people for work in the burgeoning IT sector.

Opposite: *Fishing is an important but declining sector of the Irish Republic's economy.*
Below: *The orange, white and green tricouleur is the banner of the Republic of Ireland.*

GOVERNMENT AND ECONOMY

Ireland is a democratically governed republic. Its Parliament has a 60-member upper house, the **Seanad**, which is a mix of elected and appointed members, and 166-member lower house, the **Dail**, with members elected from 41 constituencies. The head of state is the **President**. This post is largely ceremonial, but some presidents have successfully influenced the government on key issues. Day to day political power is held by the Taoiseach (prime minister). The Dail is elected by a system of proportional representation which apportions votes very fairly, but frequently leaves no one party with a commanding majority. As a result, Irish politics are characterized by minority governments, coalitions, and the art of the political deal. In 1998, six parties – Fianna Fail, Fine Gael, Labour, Progressive Democrats, Democratic Left and the Greens – were represented in the Dail, with **Fianna Fail** under Taoiseach **Bertie Ahern** forming the government.

By the summer of 1999, plans for the new Northern Ireland Assembly were in jeopardy as Ulster Unionists refused to take part unless the IRA began 'decommissioning' its weapons. This the IRA and Sinn Fein refused to do, and the peace process invited by the Good Friday agreement seemed in danger of stalling completely. Ultimate power still rests with the Northern Ireland Minister in the British Cabinet, and the **Queen** remains the **Head of State** (though not in the eyes of the nationalist community). Seventeen MPs from Northern Ireland sit in the UK parliament at Westminster. In autumn 1999 the main parties to the Good Friday agreement met once again to review its progress. In 2005 Sinn Fein/IRA agreed to decommissioning, and in 2007 the Democratic Unionist Party and Sinn Fein agreed to a devolved parliament (*see* page 25).

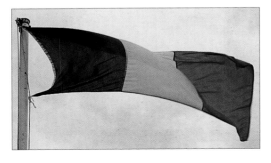

The Economy

Agriculture and **fishing** are still very important sectors of the Irish economy, but light manufacturing, electronics, the service sector and tourism all generate substantial proportions of the gross national product. Unemployment has dropped markedly in recent years and the rate of unemployment is currently one of the lowest in Europe. Nevertheless some young people still choose to go abroad in search of better-paid jobs, and earnings which they repatriate remain a significant source

of foreign income. The **cost of living** is relatively high, partly because of high rates of direct and indirect taxation on a small tax base, and partly because Ireland needs to **import** most of its raw materials, essential fuels, and many manufactured products.

The economy of Northern Ireland has been severely damaged by the Troubles, and by world economic changes which have seen the destruction of its traditional heavy industry, such as the Belfast shipyards. In the poorest parts of Belfast and Londonderry unemployment, especially among the young, is very high. Overall, unemployment accounts for around 13.5 per cent of the workforce. Employment in the manufacturing industry declined by 36 per cent between 1973 and 1990. Farming – based almost entirely on family-owned farms – employs around 57,000 people, while over 36 per cent of the workforce is in the public service sector. **Tourism** is important, with the North attracting 1.26 million visitors a year.

TOURISM

Tourism is Ireland's fourth largest source of **foreign earnings** (around 2,860 million euros a year), with more than 3.5 million visitors each year, around one million of them from continental Europe. Tourism creates some 35,000 **full-time jobs** and a great many more **seasonal jobs** (in most parts of the country the tourism industry operates at full capacity for only around half the year). In 1999 the government completed a five-year operation programme in which public and private sectors **invested** an unprecedented 830 million euros in the tourism infrastructure.

Above: *There are more under-25s in Ireland than in any other EU country.*

THE PEOPLE

The Republic of Ireland has a **population** of 4.239 million (2006 estimate). Visitors often think of Ireland as a rural society of farmers and villagers, but in fact almost 60 per cent of the population live in cities and towns.

Many of those you will meet may have worked abroad – in Britain, Europe, the USA or further afield – and large communities of Irish descent in many American and Australian cities means the Irish feel a special affinity for those countries. A **high birth rate** since World War II has given Ireland one of the youngest populations in the European Union, with more under-25s than any other EU country, a factor that gives social life (in Dublin especially) much of its youthful energy.

IRISH SLANG

Irish is spoken as a native language by only a few thousand people, but Ireland has its own rich **variations on standard English**, with a whole vocabulary of its own. Just one example is the range of expressions to describe various **stages of inebriation**, from 'dankey' (mildly drunk), 'fluthered' (seriously drunk), 'jarred' (very drunk), 'langers' (very drunk indeed) to 'scuttered' (falling down drunk). Pick up a whole new language as you go along.

The Language

English – albeit a distinctively Irish form of it – is Ireland's first language. **Irish**, sometimes also called Gaelic, fell into disuse under British rule, when its use was discouraged and sometimes banned.

Irish is a **Celtic** language closely linked to Scots Gaelic, Welsh and Breton, and reviving its use was a central priority of the Nationalist movement and of the Free State government after independence, and is a central plank in Sinn Fein's platform in Northern Ireland to this day. In the Republic Irish is taught in **schools**, and one in three Irish people now claim to speak it in addition to English (compared with one in four 30 years ago). Nobody speaks only Irish, and in most places anyone you meet is more likely to speak English than to communicate in Ireland's much older tongue. However, in the Republic, **official documents** and titles, **road signs** and **some place names** are usually presented in both Irish and English.

Religion

Catholicism and Irish Nationalism have been inextricably bound together for four centuries, and since independence the **Catholic Church** has played an extremely active part in **Irish political life**.

Religion is, of course, at the heart of **Northern Ireland's** problems, dominating politics and society almost totally. Ulster's most **hardline Protestants** regard the Catholic Church with loathing, summed up best in the intransigent slogan 'No Surrender'. The Protestants trace their religious descent back to the radical Presbyterians of the 16th and 17th centuries, and there seems to be very little likelihood that the religious fault lines which fragment Northern Ireland will vanish in the near future. Of the 1.6 million population, some 340,000 are **Presbyterian**; around 280,000 belong to the **(Protestant) Church of Ireland** and approximately 123,000 belong to **other Protestant denominations**; about 60,000 are **Methodists** and more than 606,000 are **Catholics**.

Art and Culture

The development of a distinctive national cultural scene has been regarded as an important priority in the Republic of Ireland since before independence, and a new **Department of Arts, Culture and Gaeltacht** (Irish speaking regions) was established in 1993 to foster the arts. Nowadays the **Irish Arts Council** and the **Arts Council of Northern Ireland** work very closely together on cultural projects such as touring exhibitions and performances.

YOUTH CULTURE

As a result of a 'baby boom' that came later in Ireland than elsewhere – the **birth rate** peaked in the late 1970s and early 1980s – the country now has the **youngest population in Europe**. About half the population is under 25, triggering a **clash** between the **conservative values** of the older generation and a younger generation more influenced by **international pop culture** than by the **legends and traditions** which have, until now, been such an important part of Ireland's character.

Below: *A stained-glass window at St Anne's Cathedral in Belfast.*

IRISH WRITERS

Ireland today proudly claims as its own the likes of **W B Yeats**, **James Joyce** and **Samuel Beckett**, to name but a few famous literary men born in **Dublin**. Yet most of them could hardly wait to leave for more fertile territory – Shaw, Yeats and Wilde for **London**, Beckett for **Paris** and Joyce for **Zürich**. None of them seem to have had a good word to say for the place. Dublin today meets with greater approval from contemporary Irish writers.

Literary Ireland

From the earliest Celtic times, words and music have been part of the Irish soul. Few such small countries have such rich literary traditions, from **Jonathan Swift** in the 18th century to **James Joyce** in the early 20th century and – in the 1980s and 1990s – names like Nobel Prize-winning poet **Seamus Heaney**, Booker Prize-winner **Roddy Doyle** and playwright **Brian Friel**.

'Fenian' literature, recounting the exploits of the mythical warrior king Fionn Mac Cumhaill (Finn MacCool) and his companions, flourished in the 12th and 13th century and inspired poets into the 18th and 19th centuries. Poets such as **Antoine O Reachtabra** (1784–1835) and **Micheal Og O Longain** (1779–1835) worked to keep the Irish tradition alive. Folk poetry survived into the 19th century, when the revival of Irish nationalism encouraged folklorists such as **Douglas Hyde** (later first president of the Free State) to collect and publish the work of poets such as **Diarmaid O Suilleabhain** (1760–1847), **Maire Bhui Ni Laoghaire** (1748–1830) and **Eibhlinh Dubh Ni Chonaill** (1748–1800), while later poets such as the Kerryman **Micheal O Gaoithin** (1904–74) were in direct line of literary descent from this tradition. In the 19th and 20th centuries, Irish writers such as **Peadar O Laoghaire** (1839–1920), **Seamas O Grianna** (1891–1969) and many others tried to develop the new forms influenced by contemporary European literature.

Founded in 1904 by a group which included the great Irish poet **William Butler Yeats**, the **Abbey Theatre** helped break the English stranglehold on Irish culture and provided a stage for Irish actors to perform plays by Irish playwrights to an Irish audience. Among the authors whose work it fostered were **J M Synge**, whose *The Playboy of the Western World* received a hostile reception in 1907. **Sean O'Casey**, whose *The Plough and the Stars* was produced at the Abbey, was like Synge accused of slandering the Irish people in a play which demythologized the Easter Rising, in which O'Casey had taken part. Contemporary Dublin writers include **Roddy Doyle**, whose trilogy of stories (two of which have been filmed) centres on the chaotic life of a working-class family on Dublin's Northside.

Above: *Fiddle and flute music is still alive and kicking in Ireland's pubs.* **Opposite:** *William Butler Yeats, perhaps Ireland's most famous poet.*

Contemporary Music

Music and song are everywhere in Ireland, with folk and contemporary music far outweighing the classics. World-famous rock musicians including **U2** and **Sinead O'Connor** and more recently **The Corrs** remain close to their Irish roots, while **Van Morrison**, born in Northern Ireland, has brought a distinctively Irish voice to soul and rock music. Less well-known internationally, but wellloved at home, are folk musicians like **The Dubliners**, **The Chieftains** and **Clannad**, and singer-satirist **Christy Moore**.

Classical Music and Dance

Events like the **Cork International Choral Festival**, the **Waterford Festival of Light Opera**, **Kilkenny Arts Week** and the **Guinness International Jazz Festival** in Cork have helped to put Ireland on the world music map, while the **Wexford Festival of Opera**, held each year for two weeks in October, is renowned worldwide.

TRADITIONAL MUSIC

Irish **folk music** is alive and kicking in pubs and clubs throughout the land. Some – especially in Dublin – are mainly for the benefit of visitors, with bands belting out well-loved ballads. Others are for purists bent on revitalizing traditional music. Many are venues for a fusion of Irish music with rock or world music. Best loved **traditional instruments** include the **harp**, played since the earliest times and a symbol of Irish culture; the **bodhran**, a hand-held skin drum; and the **Uillean pipes**, Ireland's version of the bagpipe.

Above: *New-style Irish cooking still loves meat and potatoes.*

Visual Arts

Leading **art galleries** include Ireland's National Gallery, the Hugh Lane Municipal Gallery, the Irish Museum of Modern Art, and the National Sculpture Factory, all in Dublin, and the Crawford Municipal Art Gallery in Cork, which houses a collection of contemporary Irish artists as well as a handful of old Masters. **Jack Butler Yeats**, son of a successful portraitist and brother of the poet William Butler Yeats, is perhaps the best-known of Irish 20th-century painters.

Arguably the most striking exhibit in the National Gallery is *The Taking of Christ*, by the Italian painter Michelangelo Merisi da Caravaggio (1573–1610). Missing for several hundred years, it was rediscovered in Dublin in 1992 and restored by the National Gallery. Contemporary painters in the 1990s, many of them producing dramatic abstracts, include **Paddy Graham**, **Sean Scully** and **Felim Egan**.

Film

Film has a strong following in Ireland, partly because state-run television has until recently offered staid programming and little choice. Video, cable and satellite TV challenge cinema's popularity, but **government support** for the film industry (through subsidies and tax breaks) is strong and Ireland attracts many international film-makers as well as producing home-grown talent of world-class quality.

Food and Drink

Traditional Irish food is best described as hearty, heavy on calories and usually based on beef or mutton, with plenty of root vegetables such as potatoes, carrots, onions and turnips, typified by dishes like **Irish stew**. Since the 1980s, however, Irish cooking, too, has changed with the times. Irish chefs have created a **new style of cookery**, based on Ireland's superb local produce – fine beef and lamb, fresh dairy products and terrific seafood from the Atlantic coasts – often cooked in a style strongly influenced by *nouvelle cuisine*.

Ireland is the home of **Guinness**, the creamy dark stout or porter which is **Ireland's national drink**. There are other porters – such as Caffrey's, Beamish's and Murphy's – but it is Guinness which rules the roost, fuelling many a high-flown literary conversation. Guinness is **exported** worldwide and brewed under licence in many parts of the world but, as any Dubliner will tell you, it is not the real thing unless it has been brewed from the water of the **River Liffey**.

Below: *A pint of plain is your only man. Guinness still rules the roost.*

2
Dublin

Dublin (also known by its Irish name, *Baile Átha Cliath*), is home to just over a million people and covers an area of only 388km² (150 sq miles). One of the city's greatest charms is that most of its attractions are packed cheek by jowl in the city centre, only a few minutes' walk from each other.

Ireland's capital is a place of rapid modernization side by side with living history. Dublin is bisected by the **River Liffey**, flowing roughly west to east into Dublin Bay, with the historic heart of the city lying just south of the river, where a series of riverside streets bear names reminiscent of a mercantile past – Victoria Quay, Usher's Quay, Merchant's Quay, Wellington Quay, Aston Quay, Burgh Quay, George's Quay and City Quay. Merchant shipping no longer sails up the Liffey right into the heart of the city, but in Dublin's 18th-century heyday this **waterfront** bristled with masts. Central Dublin is dotted with **historic buildings**, some dating from the foundation of the city by the Norsemen in the 10th century.

Nine **bridges**, two of which are historic landmarks, cross the Liffey in the city centre. The three elegantly arched spans of O'Connell Bridge date from 1790 and it still carries most of Dublin's cross-river traffic. Originally named Carlisle Bridge, it was renamed after independence in honour of 19th-century Home Rule campaigner Daniel O'Connell. The Liffey Bridge, or Ha'penny Bridge, an elegant cast-iron footbridge, dates from 1816 and takes its nickname from the halfpenny toll which was once charged to cross it.

DON'T MISS

★★★ Christ Church Cathedral: ancient cathedral with historic tombs.
★★★ St Patrick's Cathedral: pageant of history in gracious 800-year-old building.
★★★ Guinness Brewery: home of Ireland's most famous product.
★★ Kilmainham Gaol: eerie memorial to the dead of Ireland's independence struggle.
★★ Dublin Castle: Viking and British relics.
★★ Phoenix Park: historic buildings, riverside walks and a fine zoo.

Opposite: *The River Liffey flows through the very heart of Dublin.*

TOP TEN THINGS TO DO

- Get a taste for **Guinness** at the Hop Store.
- Try **Irish Whiskey** at Jameson's Distillery.
- Follow **James Joyce's** footsteps on a guided walk.
- Sing along at a traditional **Irish music pub**.
- Trace your **Irish ancestry**.
- Spend a day at the **races** or a **Gaelic football** game.
- Take a leisurely walk in the **Dublin Mountains**.
- Go skinny-dipping at **Forty Foot beach**.
- Wander through the lively **street markets**.
- Dine out on fabulous **fresh seafood**.

Below: *Trinity College has educated generations of Irish students.*

SOUTH OF THE LIFFEY
Trinity College ★★★

This 16ha (40-acre) complex was founded by Queen Elizabeth I in 1592 and is now the campus of the **University of Ireland**. The cobbled squares and the manicured lawns date from as early as the 17th century, and there are additions from every era. The greatest treasure in the College's **Colonnades Gallery** is the **Book of Kells**, a manuscript of the four gospels which dates from the 8th century and is one of the oldest surviving documents of early Western Christendom. The text is richly decorated with complex Celtic abstract designs, and fantastic creatures and figures. **Illuminated manuscripts** taken from the ancient monasteries of Durrow and Armagh are also on display, along with one of the very earliest **Irish harps**. The Colonnades Gallery is open daily 09:30–17:00.

Trinity College also houses **The Dublin Experience**, a striking audiovisual show which tells the story of Dublin from the earliest times to the present day. Open mid-May to mid-October, daily 10:00–17:00.

Bank of Ireland
(Old Irish Parliament) ★★★

Constructed in 1729 as the seat of the Irish Parliament and now housing the headquarters of the Bank of Ireland, this structure was rebuilt by **Francis Johnston**, Dublin's greatest Georgian architect, after the Act of Union in 1800. The chamber of the Irish **House of Lords**, an oak-panelled hall decorated with 18th-century **tapestries**, is brightly lit by a beautiful glittering 18th-century **chandelier** made of more than 1200 pieces of cut crystal. The building is open Monday–Friday 10:00–16:00, Thursday 10:00–17:00. Guided tours Tuesday 10:00, 11:30 and 13:45.

Left: *The Temple Bar district, with its many pubs and clubs, is the hub of Dublin's nightlife.*

Temple Bar ★★★

The Temple Bar district, Dublin's 'Cultural Quarter' on the south bank of the Liffey between Wellington Quay and Dame Street, is a block of **cobbled streets** laid out in the 18th century. Its buildings have been restored and streets have been pedestrianized to create an attractive **shopping** and **entertainment** district. Temple Bar is also a **nightlife centre**, with many theatres, cinemas, clubs and pubs, and the biggest choice of restaurants in Dublin.

Temple Bar Information Centre, Curved Street/ Eustace Street, is open June–August, weekdays 09:00– 19:00, Saturday 11:00–19:00, Sunday 12:00–18:00; September–May, weekdays 09:30–18:00, Saturday 12:00–18:00.

Dublin Castle ★★★

The castle has been added to and altered over centuries. The first stronghold on the site was a **Viking fortress**, but the oldest parts of the present building date from between 1208 and 1220. Part of the even older Viking stronghold can be seen in the medieval **Undercroft** section of the castle, which also houses a restaurant and heritage centre. Also within its walls are the gracious **State Apartments**, used on state and diplomatic occasions, of which **St Patrick's Hall**, with its high painted ceiling, is the most imposing; and the **Church of the Most Holy Trinity**. Open Monday–Friday 10:00–16:45, Sunday 14:00–16:45.

THOMAS MOORE

Educated at Trinity College, Thomas Moore (1779–1852) was one of Ireland's best loved poets and lyricists. He travelled widely in Europe and the USA and wrote many **poems** and **airs** inspired by his homeland, the best known of which are contained in the collection of *Irish Melodies* he published between 1807 and 1834. He was a close friend of **Lord Byron**, whose memoirs he was given to publish but found so shocking he instead destroyed them, thus depriving posterity of a rich source of titillation.

Above: *Dublin Castle was for generations the symbol of British imperialism.*
Opposite: *The beautiful medieval interior of St Patrick's Cathedral.*
Below: *Christ Church Cathedral, one of Dublin's larger monuments.*

Christ Church Cathedral ★★★

The first cathedral on this site was built by the Christian Viking king Sitric Silkenbeard, but the building you see today was endowed by the Norman Earl of Pembroke, **Richard de Clare** ('Strongbow'), who had it built after his conquest of Dublin in 1170. It was restored in 1871, when several Victorian Gothic features were added. The oldest parts of the church are the **south transept**, which dates from around 1180, and the **crypt**, dating from 1172. The cathedral is open daily 09:45–17:00 (18:00 in June and August).

Dublinia ★★

Developed by Dublin's **Medieval Trust**, Dublinia – linked by footbridge to Christ Church Cathedral – brings four centuries of Dublin's past to life in a series of living tableaux and dioramas. High points include life-size reconstructions of part of the 13th-century Wood Quay and the interior of a 15th-century merchant's house. Displays of genuine artefacts from the **National Museum of Ireland** give insight into work, commerce and leisure in medieval times. Open April to end September, daily 10:00–17:00; October–March, Monday–Saturday 11:00–16:00, Sunday 10:00–16:00.

NEW QUARTER

In 1999 Dublin Corporation handed over 'Dublin's Bedlam', the 200-year-old **Grangegorman Asylum**, for development with the aim of creating an exciting new academic urban quarter in the heart of the city. Some 12ha (30 acres) of the 26ha (65-acre) site is zoned as open space, and plans call for the re-opening of the former Broadstone suburban railway line, now closed, as part of the city's rapid transit system.

St Stephen's Green and Around

This area of South Dublin, between Trinity College and the southern sector of the Grand Canal which rings central Dublin, contains many of the city's best-preserved **Georgian buildings** and a number of fine museums. **Grafton Street**, which runs between Trinity College and St Stephen's Green, was an elegant residential area in the 18th century. Pedestrianized in the 1980s, it has Dublin's most expensive **shops** and in summer is often populated with **street musicians** and **entertainers**. St Stephen's Green is one of the most attractive **parks** in Dublin.

St Patrick's Cathedral ★★★

Dublin's second medieval cathedral, at Patrick's Close, stands on the site where, it is claimed, Ireland's patron saint baptized his converts to Christianity. The first church on the spot was built in AD450, and replaced in 1191 by the present building. The cathedral was restored in the 1860s, so what you now see – an attractive building in light-coloured limestone with a taller, slimmer tower than the rival Christ Church Cathedral – is a Victorian reinterpretation of the original Norman building. The **West Tower**, which was added in 1370, contains the second-largest carillon in Ireland. Within the cathedral are **Celtic tombstones**, and the transepts are graced by the faded banners of Irish regiments. **Jonathan Swift**, the author of *Gulliver's Travels*, was Dean of St Patrick's from 1713–45 and is buried here in the cathedral. Open Monday–Friday 09:00–18:00, Saturday 09:00–17:00, Sunday 10:00–15:00.

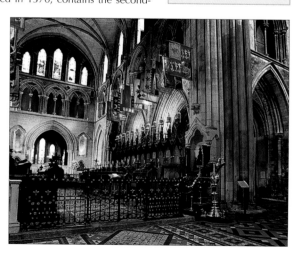

CLASSICAL ARCHITECTURE

The first Classical buildings in Ireland date from the late 17th century, among them the Royal Hospital in Dublin, designed by **Sir William Robinson**. Later, in the early 1700s, Palladian country houses began to be built, notably by the architects **Sir Edward Lovett Pearce** (designer of the old Parliament House) and **Richard Castle** (who designed Leinster House). In the late 18th century the neo-Classical style became fashionable. Its greatest exponent was **James Gandon** (1743–1823), who designed the Custom House and the Four Courts. Still later, **Francis Johnston** (1760–1829), architect of the General Post Office, gave Dublin many of its fine Georgian streets and squares.

Right: *Despite the ravages of recent development, remnants of Georgian Dublin, like these elegant doors, survive.*

Shaw Birthplace ★★★

The birthplace of **George Bernard Shaw** (1856–1950), at 33 Synge Street, is decorated and furnished in the style of the mid-19th century, with a stuffily furnished and adorned front parlour, the children's bedroom, upstairs drawing room and a tidy, peaceful Victorian back garden. Open May–September, Monday–Friday 10:00–13:00 and 14:00–17:00, Saturday–Sunday 14:00–17:00.

Newman House ★★★

Two beautiful **Georgian townhouses**, at 85–86 St Stephen's Green, restored in 1989, offer the finest recreation of the elegance of wealthy 18th-century Dublin. During the 19th century the buildings housed the **Catholic University** founded by **Cardinal Newman**. A guided tour helps to put the buildings in their historic context. Open Tuesday–Friday 14:00–17:00.

National Library ★★

This grand library just north of St Stephen's Green is the place to start seeking your **Irish ancestry**. The library has an enormous **archive**, including near-complete runs of every newspaper and magazine ever printed in Ireland and a huge **reference section**. Open Monday–Wednesday 10:00–21:00, Thursday–Friday 10:00–17:00, Saturday 10:00–13:00.

National Museum of Ireland ★★★

The high points of the National Museum's collection include the magnificently decorated **Ardagh Chalice** and the intricately worked golden **Tara Brooch** and **Cross of Cong**, priceless relics of the early Christian era. **Ireland's Gold**, another breathtaking display, features gorgeously made prehistoric gold artefacts. Open Tuesday–Saturday 10:00–17:00, and Sunday 14:00–17:00.

Above: *The ancient Irish monarchs amassed treasuries of rich golden ornaments like these.*

National Gallery of Ireland ★★★

The National Gallery collection includes almost 2500 paintings, more than 5000 drawings and watercolours, and over 3000 prints, with works from every school of **European painting**, and the world's best collection of **Irish painters**. Open Monday–Saturday 09:30–17:30, Thursday 09:30–20:30, Sunday 12:00–17:30. Guided tours Saturday 15:00, Sunday 14:30, 15:15 and 16:00.

Number Twenty Nine ★★★

Owned by the Electricity Supply Board, this historic house situated at 29 Lower Fitzwilliam Street, Dublin 2, is furnished and decorated as a typical home of a better-off Dublin family of the late 18th and early 19th century. The reception rooms are furnished either with **period pieces** or finely made replicas, and the carpets and curtains, paint and plaster are all in keeping with the period. The family bedrooms, nursery and play-rooms with their **19th-century toys** will fascinate children as well as adults. Open Tuesday–Saturday 10:00–17:00, Sunday 13:00–17:00.

TRACING YOUR ROOTS

If you want to track down your Irish ancestors, a good place to start is **Dublin's National Library**, with its huge collection of newspapers and magazines that may hold clues to your roots, such as birth and wedding announcements. The **Irish Genealogical Office** is attached to the National Library, and offers a consultancy service on ancestry tracing.

Right: *O'Connell Street,
north Dublin's main
thoroughfare.*

NORTH OF THE LIFFEY

Many of Dublin's most substantial **public buildings**
stand north of the Liffey, a part of the city which first
became fashionable in the late 17th and early 18th
centuries. This is the busiest part of the modern city,
with **shopping** streets, commercial offices and open-air
markets. The Custom House is a reminder that the
north bank was once busy with **shipping**, and the former docklands next to it have been rejuvenated as
Ireland's new **financial services** centre. The area is
bisected by **O'Connell Street**, the widest and most
important traffic route through the city centre, which
crosses the river by the eight-lane **O'Connell Bridge**.

General Post Office ★

Designed by **Francis Johnston** and completed in 1818,
the GPO on O'Connell Street has a portico surmounted
by symbolic statues of Mercury (messenger of the gods
and therefore patron of postal services), Fidelity and
Hibernia (Ireland). It was the hub of the **Easter Rising** of
1916, when a group of Irish volunteers held out for six
days under British bombardment. They are commemor-
ated by a statue of the legendary Irish hero **Cuchulainn**
in the main hall. Open Monday–Saturday 08:00–20:00.

Dublin Writers Museum ★★★

Housed in a grand 18th-century townhouse at 18/19 Parnell Square North, this museum is filled with fascinating personal memorabilia, manuscripts, first editions and portraits of Irish writers and storytellers. Pride of place is given to Ireland's Nobel Prizewinners, **George Bernard Shaw**, **W B Yeats**, **Samuel Beckett** (all of whom, ironically, spent more time away from Ireland than in it), and most recently also to **Seamus Heaney**, winner of the Nobel Prize for Literature in 1998. Open Monday–Saturday 10:00–17:00, Sundays and public holidays 11:00–17:00. Late opening until 18:00 Monday–Friday, June–August.

James Joyce Cultural Centre ★★

Located at 5 North Great St George's Street, off Parnell Street, Dublin 1, this 18th-century townhouse has been restored as a shrine to the author of *Ulysses* and *Dubliners*. The centre aims to increase interest in Joyce's life and work – a welcome change from the not-so-distant past when *Ulysses* was banned in Ireland because it was considered obscene. Published in 1922, Joyce's hefty tome recounts, through the stream-of-consciousness style of writing which the author pioneered, the events of a single day – 16 June 1904 – through the eyes of the book's central character, **Leopold Bloom**, and a few other protagonists. Today 16 June is celebrated as 'Bloomsday' in Dublin, with readings from *Ulysses*, re-enactments of events in the book, and actors playing the parts of the Joycean characters wandering around the streets in costume. Open Monday–Saturday 09:30–17:00, Sunday 12:30–17:00.

PATRICK KAVANAGH

Patrick Kavanagh (1904–67) is second only to Yeats in his influence on Ireland's **poetry**. The son of a small farmer, he left school at the age of 13. His poetry, dealing as it does with the harsher realities of **rural life**, was shaped by his background and his un-compromising personality. His first book, *Ploughman and Other Poems*, was published in 1936, but despite the acclaim he received thereafter his great talent failed to bring him a comfortable living.

Below: *James Joyce spent most of his working life abroad, but his library is preserved at the James Joyce Cultural Centre.*

IRISH WHISKEY

Christian monks brought distillation to Ireland in the 6th century AD, perhaps from the Arab world, where stills were used to make perfume. Feeling the need of a warming dram in the chill climate of their new home, they invented *uisce beatha* (pronounced ik'ke ba'ha) – the **Water of Life**. Ireland has not been the same since. Irish whiskeys are made from **malted barley** dried in a **closed kiln**, not over an open fire like the barley in Scotch whisky. As a result, the Irish version lacks the smoky flavour of Scotch malts.

Opposite: *The Royal Hospital Gardens and Phoenix Park, Kilmainham.* **Below:** *A fine selection of Irish whiskey on show.*

Custom House ★

The Custom House was designed by **James Gandon** (who was also responsible for two other fine buildings dating from the late 18th and early 19th century – the Four Courts and the King's Inns) and completed in 1791. Just east of O'Connell Bridge, its superbly proportioned **Doric portico** is flanked by carved stone busts, each representing one of Ireland's great rivers. The building is crowned by a 38m high (125ft) **copper dome** atop which stands a **bronze statue** representing Commerce. Visitors' Centre open mid-March to October Monday–Friday 10:00–12:30, Saturday–Sunday 14:00–17:00.

The Four Courts ★★

Like the Custom House, this splendid 18th-century courthouse on Inn's Quay was designed by **James Gandon**. Occupied by anti-Free State rebels during the Civil War, it was bombarded and heavily damaged by Government troops. Restoration was completed in 1932 and today the building is the seat of the **Irish Supreme and High Courts**. The entrance hall, with its soaring dome, is open to visitors Monday–Saturday 10:00–17:00, Sundays and public holidays 11:30–18:00. Late opening until 19:00 Monday–Friday, June–August.

Old Jameson Distillery ★★★

The former Jameson's Whiskey warehouse on Bow Street has been converted into an exhibition centre with a **model distillery** and antique copper pot stills and equipment, bottles and labels. A 15-minute audiovisual presentation tells the story of how *uisce beatha* is made, and admission includes a glass of whiskey in the adjoining **Ball of Malt Bar**, which is decorated with fine, old, frosted and gilt advertising mirrors collected from some of Dublin's vanished Victorian bars. You can also go on to learn to be a **qualified whiskey taster**, with a certificate to prove it. Open daily 09:30–18:00.

PHOENIX PARK AND KILMAINHAM

Phoenix Park is claimed to be the largest city park in Europe, offering a year-round respite from the bustle of central Dublin. Just 3km (2 miles) west of the centre, it is a favourite with joggers and other **sports** players and watchers, with facilities for Gaelic football, hurling, polo, cricket, cycling and athletics. The residences of the **President of Ireland** and the **US Ambassador** are also situated amid its 709ha (1752-acre) expanse of lawns and leafy woodland. Established by the **Duke of Ormonde** in 1662 as a deer preserve, the park still has a resident herd of 300 **fallow deer**. The River Liffey and the main road parallel to it form the southern boundary of the park and separate it from Kilmainham, south of the river. This **residential suburb** is the site of two buildings which for very different reasons are virtually national shrines: Kilmainham Gaol and the Guinness Breweries.

Kilmainham Gaol ★★★

A towered gateway is the landmark for this grim prison at Kilmainham and shrine to the heroes of the Irish struggle for independence. Once the main prison in Ireland, it is now a memorial to men like **Robert Emmett**, **Charles Stewart Parnell**, **Eamon de Valera** and **James Connolly**, all of whom were incarcerated here. Some, like Parnell and de Valera, were fortunate enough to walk out again. Others, like the leaders of the **Easter Rising**, were executed in Kilmainham's prison yard. A symbol of British rule, Kilmainham is a monument to the most tragic moments in Irish history, including the failed rebellions of 1798, 1803, 1848, 1867 and 1916. A visit to the gaol includes an informative guided tour and an audiovisual presentation. Open April–September, daily 09:30–17:00; October–March, Monday–Saturday 09:30–16:00, Sunday 10:00–17:00.

HURLING

Hurling looks lethal – and sometimes is. A distant relative of hockey, the game is played with a paddle-like wooden stick. Players use its broad head to catch, balance or throw the ball with great force. It's a **fast moving game**, and in the flurry of whirling sticks it seems amazing that any player emerges unscathed. It is also a game with a long **history** – Irish legends and early written and pictorial sources show that it was played more than a thousand years ago.

Guinness Storehouse ★★★

Guinness Brewery was founded in 1759 and the **museum** celebrating Ireland's favourite brew – 10 million glasses are produced daily around the world – is situated next to the **historic brewery** in a handsome 19th-century building at James's Gate, together with the World of Guinness exhibition, an audiovisual show, a transport museum and a bar in which to acquire this most Irish of tastes. Open daily 09:30–17:00 (until 19:00 in July and August). www.guinness-storehouse.com

Above: *The Hop Store celebrates Guinness, Ireland's favourite tipple.*
Opposite: *The harbour at Dun Laoighaire, used by yachts, fishing vessels and Irish Sea ferries.*

Irish Museum of Modern Art/Royal Hospital Kilmainham ★★

A fine collection of 20th-century international and Irish artists is housed in a former military veterans' hospice at Military Road, Kilmainham. Built in 1684 and in use until 1927, the building is architecturally similar to Les Invalides in Paris, and is the oldest intact **Classical building** in Ireland. Features worth looking at include its grand **banqueting hall** and wood-panelled **Baroque chapel**. Open Tuesday–Saturday 10:00–17:30, Sunday 12:00–17:30.

SOUTH DUBLIN SUBURBS AND DUBLIN BAY COAST

Beyond the southern crescent of the tree-lined **Grand Canal**, built in the 18th century to connect the city with the Shannon, Ireland's most important river, lie the suburbs of the city's **green belt**. Dublin Bay sweeps in a 13km (8-mile) crescent from the mouth of the River Liffey south to Dalkey headland and along its coast. Several small towns have merged into a suburban seaside strip stretching south to Dun Laoghaire, the main port for ferries to England and Wales, and beyond to the beaches of Killiney Bay.

IRELAND'S LARGEST CITIES

Dublin (pop. 915,000)
Belfast (279,237)
Cork (174,000)
Derry (95,381)
Limerick (75,000)
Galway (51,000)
Waterford (42,000)
Dundalk (30,000)

Ballsbridge

This old South Dublin residential area is best known as the location of **Landsdowne Road Stadium**, Ireland's international rugby football stadium, which comes into its own each spring when Ireland's rugby team – with players from the republic and from Northern Ireland – pits its skills in international matches against Scotland, England, Wales, France and Italy.

Booterstown

A quiet suburb close to the Irish Sea, Booterstown's main point of interest is its 4ha (10 acre) wildfowl reserve. The **Booterstown Marsh Bird Sanctuary** on the outskirts of the city is maintained by the Irish Wildbird Conservancy and the National Trust for Ireland. Keen birders can get close to a variety of common and rare ducks, geese, grebes and wading birds using waterside hides.

Monkstown

Monkstown overlooks Dublin Bay, with a string of bathing places along its sweep of beach. The **Culturlann na hEireann** (Irish Cultural Institute) in the village is the centre of *Comhaltas Ceoltoiri Eireann*, the cultural movement which does most to sustain Irish folk culture. It is open in summer (June to end August) for performances of traditional music, singing and dance.

Dun Laoghaire

Dun Laoghaire (pronounced Dun Leary) is claimed to have been the seat of a 5th-century king named Laoghaire, converted to Christianity by St Patrick. In the 19th century it was renamed Kingstown, in honour of King George IV's visit to Ireland in 1821. It reverted to its Irish name after independence. Its **harbour**, built in the mid-19th century, is wider than a mile across, more than ample for the Irish Sea ferry fleet which operates from here to British ports and for the

VIKING DUBLIN

The **Dublin Norse** made the city one of the wealthiest trade ports in Western Europe, through commerce with the Baltic, North Sea and Mediterranean. Gold and silver coins and glass-ware from **Scandinavia** found on the site of Viking Dublin indicate trade with that part of the world in the 10th century. Later finds show that by the 12th century Dublin was trading with **England** and **Normandy**. In the 11th and 12th centuries Dublin was a substantial town, surrounded by stone walls and ruled by Christian Norse-Irish kings who inter-married with local nobles.

flotilla of yachts moored offshore from the clubhouse of the **Royal Irish Yacht Club**.

Housed in the former Mariners' Church, built in 1837, the **National Maritime Museum** is run by the Maritime Institute of Ireland. The museum's collection includes lighthouse equipment and a flotilla of ship models. It is open, Saturday–Sunday 13:00–17:00.

Sandycove ★

Sandycove, located only about 1km (0.5 mile) south of Dun Laoghaire's massive East Pier, has a pretty **yacht harbour** and a small beach between rocky headlands. **Forty Foot Cove** is a bit longer than its name suggests, and is said to have been named after the Fortieth Regiment of Foot (infantry) who were garrisoned nearby during the 19th century.

James Joyce Tower and Museum ★★★

The rather squat round tower overlooking the sea at Sandycove is one of a series of Martello towers, identical small fortresses built at strategic landing places around the coasts of Ireland and mainland Britain in 1804 to defend the countries against the threat of a French invasion. A century later, this particular one gained a place in literary history when **James Joyce** stayed here as a guest of the writer **Oliver St John Gogarty**, later making it the setting for the first chapter of his most famous novel, *Ulysses*, published in 1922. It now houses a **museum** dedicated to Joyce's life and works, and it contains a treasury of fascinating Joycean memorabilia. Open March to October, Monday–Saturday 10:00–13:00 and 14:00–17:00, and Sunday 14:00–18:00.

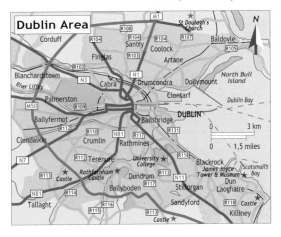

Dalkey ★

With its two pretty harbours, Dalkey still feels like a real seaside village. In medieval times it was an important seaport, defended by ramparts of **Archibald's Castle**, which, together with Goat's Castle are the only survivors of that time. Also on Castle Street, next to Archibald's Castle, is the shell of the medieval **St Begnet's Church**, surrounded by a small graveyard full of eroded gravestones whose dates reach back to the Norman era.

About 1km (0.5 mile) offshore from Coliemore Harbour the walls of a **Martello tower**, twin to the James Joyce Tower at Sandycove, rise from the highest point of Dalkey Island to command Dalkey Sound. The tiny island is a **bird sanctuary** and there are several boat trips a day in summer from Coliemore Harbour.

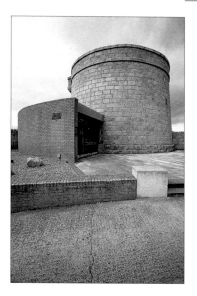

Killiney Bay And Killiney Hill ★

Killiney Bay is a strikingly beautiful sweep of sheltered beach. Overlooking it, Killiney Hill is one of the Dublin area's most beautiful landscaped parks, with a signposted **nature trail** and a scattering of decorative **follies** and **monuments** dating from the 18th and 19th centuries.

Rathfarnham ★

Some 8km (5 miles) inland from Killiney, Rathfarnham stands on the River Dodder, on the very edge of Dublin, and is the starting point for one of the most worthwhile walks in Ireland, the **Wicklow Way**.

Built in 1585 as an archbishop's residence, **Rathfarnham Castle** was for many years used as a Jesuit college. The interior is extravagantly Rococo, with remarkable stucco friezes and ceilings and grandly spacious rooms. Next to it is **Cromwell's Barn**, a fortified 16th-century barn which the Parliamentary commander Oliver Cromwell is reputed to have used as headquarters in 1649. Open May–October 09:30–17:30.

Above: *Martello Tower at Sandycove, where Joyce and St John Gogarty sought literary inspiration.*

OLIVER ST JOHN GOGARTY

Oliver St John Gogarty (1878–1957), one of Ireland's wittiest **writers**, trained as a surgeon and later wrote volumes of fiction, poetry and reminiscence. His best known work, *As I was Going Down Sackville Street*, is a celebration of Dublin. He was a member of the Irish Free State's first **Senate**, but later left Ireland, first for England, then for America.

Above: *The Botanical Gardens at Glasnevin are a blaze of colour in spring and summer.*

The small **Pearse Museum** in Rathfarnham commemorates Padraig Pearse's work as a teacher, author and poet. Pearse (1879– 1916) was prominent in the Irish Republican Brotherhood and he was executed for his part as commander of the rebel forces in the Easter Rising of 1916. Open November–January, daily 10:00– 13:00, 14:00–16:00; February–April, September–October, daily 10:00– 13:00, 14:00–17:00; May–August, daily 10:00–13:00, 14:00–17:30.

NORTH DUBLIN COAST

Like the Grand Canal in South Dublin, the **Royal Canal** flowing into the River Liffey forms a very convenient boundary between central Dublin and its northern suburbs. The Northside suburbs contain one of Dublin's working-class heartlands, where many city-centre slum-dwellers have been rehoused in the rebuilding of the city since the 1950s. In sharp contrast, the North Dublin seaside suburb of Howth, standing on a peninsula at the northern point of Dublin Bay, is Dublin's most conspicuously wealthy neighbourhood.

National Botanic Gardens, Glasnevin ★★★

Straddling the **River Tolka**, Glasnevin is primarily a residential suburb, worth visiting for Dublin's outstanding botanic gardens, which rival the world-famous Kew Gardens in London.

The gardens cover about 20ha (49 acres). Flowering shrubs and bushes ensure a blaze of colour for much of the year. The **Great Palm House**, built in 1884, is yet to be restored to its former grandeur. The gardens contain more than 20,000 plant species, from rare orchids and tree ferns to 30m (100ft) Californian sequoias. Open in summer, Monday–Saturday 09:00–18:00, Sunday 10:00–18:00; in winter, daily 10:00–16:30.

CHILLY DIP

Only the brave celebrate Christmas Day with an early-morning dip at **Forty Foot**, the small beach below James Joyce's tower at Sandycove, where **skinny-dipping** (formerly men-only but now open to women too) has been a tradition for decades. Few stay in the chilly Irish Sea for more than a few minutes, and when honour is satisfied, a drop of whiskey helps to fend off pneumonia.

Clontarf ★

Now a pleasant seaside suburb, Clontarf was the ancient site of **Brian Boru's** victory over a Norse and Irish alliance in 1014. The exact location of the battlefield is, however, unknown.

North Bull Wall and Island is a 900m long (984yd) breakwater constructed during the early 19th century. North Bull Wall created an island of sand dunes and salt marshes on its north side. Part of North Bull Island is a **bird sanctuary** and a UNESCO **Biosphere Reserve**. Up to 40,000 birds – including rare Brent greese – shelter and nest here, their numbers boosted in winter by tens of thousands of Arctic migrants. Unique wetlands also foster rare plant species including sea lavender, sea aster and glasswort. Open daily.

Howth ★

Built on and around **Howth Head**, a craggy, 170m (558ft) headland jutting into the Irish Sea and protecting Dublin Bay from northerly gales, Howth started life as a fishing harbour in medieval times but has become Dublin's wealthiest neighbourhood. There are fine views in all directions from the top of Howth Head. A 19th-century **Martello tower**, built to protect Ireland against French invasion during the Napoleonic Wars, guards the harbour, which is overlooked by the ruins of **St Mary's Abbey**, dating from 1253.

Howth Castle Gardens are best visited from May to early June to see the 2000 varieties of rhododendron in all their scarlet, crimson, pink, white and purple splendour. The gardens also contain a ruined 18th-century square tower, **Corr Castle**, and a Neolithic barrow locally known as **Aideen's Grave**. Open daily from 08:00 to sunset.

Below: *Fishing boats and fishermen's houses at West Pier, Howth Harbour.*

Dublin at a Glance

BEST TIMES TO VISIT

Dublin can be visited year-round, but **summer** and **autumn** are usually more pleasant. Dublin has mild wet winters and temperate wet summers – always be prepared for rain. Heavy snow is rare in the city even in midwinter, and summer temperatures rarely reach above 20°C (68°F). There are four distinct seasons: spring (April–May), summer (June–September), autumn (October–November) and winter (December–March). July and August are the hottest months, January and February the coldest.

GETTING THERE

Frequent flights from most major British cities including London, Birmingham, Manchester, Glasgow and Edinburgh. There are also flights from most major European capitals and key gateway cities in the USA and Canada.
By Sea: Daily ferries to Dublin and Dun Laoghaire from Holyhead in Wales.
By Road: Main north road A1 connects Dublin with Belfast and the North.
By Rail: Several trains daily between Dublin and Belfast, and frequent rail services to other regional cities in the Republic of Ireland.

GETTING AROUND

Highly compact and walkable, Dublin is easiest explored on foot. Public transport includes

buses and a light **rail** line. Buses run between 06:00 and 23:30. Dublin Area Rapid Transport (**DART**) trains run on a 36km (22-mile) line along Dublin Bay from Howth to Bray, with efficient connections between city centre and residential suburbs. Main DART stations are Connolly Station for connections to mainline trains, Tara Street and Pearse Street for south central Dublin. Enquiries: tel: (01) 836-6222. Main **taxi** ranks are at Amiens Street (Connolly Station), O'Connell Street and St Stephen's Green.

WHERE TO STAY

Dublin has a range of places to stay to suit all budgets, but in summer the city is crowded and advance reservations are advised. **Dublin Tourism**, Suffolk Street, operates a year-round computerized accommodation booking service (*see* Tourist Reservations under Useful Contacts for details), and publishes accommodation guides including the *Dublin Accommodation Guide, Be Our Guest Guide*, and guides to hostels, camping holidays, farm holidays and country homes.

LUXURY
Le Méridien Shelbourne, 27 St Stephen's Green, Dublin 2, tel: (01) 663-4500, fax: (01) 661-6006. One of the finest hotels in the city, with luxurious, individually deco-

rated rooms, two bars and fine Irish restaurant.
Berkeley Court Hotel, Lansdowne Road, Ballsbridge, Dublin 4, tel: (01) 665-3200, fax: (01) 661-7238. Five-star with two restaurants, two bars, business centre and mini gym.
Conrad Hotel Dublin, Earlsfort Terrace, Dublin 2, tel: (01) 602-8990, fax: (01) 676-5424. Luxury 191-room hotel, two restaurants and Irish pub.
Trinity Capital Hotel, Pearse Street, Dublin 2, tel: (01) 648-1000, fax: (01) 648-1010. Opened in 2000, this central hotel boasts beautiful interior design and an elegant bar area.

MID-RANGE
Blooms, 6 Anglesea Street, Temple Bar, Dublin 2, tel: (01) 671-5622, fax: (01) 671-5997. Intimate hotel with 86 rooms. Good base for central Dublin.
Jurys Inn Christchurch, Christchurch Place, Dublin 8, tel: (01) 454-0000, fax: (01) 454-0012. Modern three-star hotel opposite cathedral.
Davenport Hotel, Merrion Square, Dublin 2, tel: (01) 607-3500, fax: (01) 661-5663. Built in 1863 as a church, it has striking period façade, comfortable in-room facilities, *en-suite* rooms with colour TV.
Ariel House, 50–54 Lansdowne Road, Ballsbridge, Dublin 4, tel: (01) 668-5512, fax: (01) 668-5845. Fine four-star guesthouse in restored Victorian mansion.

Dublin at a Glance

BUDGET

Fitzwilliam Guesthouse,
41 Upper Fitzwilliam Street,
Dublin 2, tel: (01) 662-5155,
fax: (01) 676-7488. Three-star
guesthouse near St Stephen's
Green; rooms have *en-suite*
shower, colour TV, direct-dial
telephone and hairdryers.
Barry's Hotel, 1–2 Great
Denmark Street, Dublin 1, tel:
(01) 874-9407, fax: (01) 874-
6508. Comfortable two-star
hotel within walking distance
of Dublin's main attractions.
Clifden Guesthouse, 32
Gardiner Place, Dublin 1, tel:
(01) 874-6364, fax: (01) 874-
6122. Two-star guesthouse in
Georgian townhouse.

WHERE TO EAT

The city's best restaurants com-
pare with any in Europe, many
specializing in Irish seafood,
game, beef, lamb, pork and
dairy. Dublin pubs offer a lunch
and dinner menu. The Irish
Tourist Board annually updates
the *Dining in Ireland Guide*.

LUXURY

The Grey Door, 22–23 Upper
Pembroke Street, Dublin 2,
tel: (01) 676-3286.
Recommended, long
established, Irish food.
Alexandra, Conrad Hotel,
Earlsfort Terrace, Dublin 2, tel:
(01) 676-5555. Gourmet restaurant in a top Dublin hotel.
27 Green, Shelbourne Hotel,
27 St Stephen's Green, Dublin
2, tel: (01) 663-4720. Specializes in the best Irish produce.

MID-RANGE

**Ante Room Seafood Res-
taurant**, 18 Lower Baggot
Street, Dublin 2, tel: (01) 662-
5098. Good value, seafood,
near St Stephen's Green.
Harbourmaster Restaurant,
Old Dock Offices, Custom
House Dock, Dublin 1, tel: (01)
670-1688. Fish and lobster.

BUDGET

O'Shea's Merchant, 12 Lower
Bridge Street, Dublin 8, tel: (01)
679-3797. Lively pub with
soup and snacks, traditional
music and dancing nightly.
Castle Vaults Bistro, Lower
Castle Yard, Dublin Castle,
Dublin 2, tel: (01) 677-0678.
Good cheap lunches.

SHOPPING

Best buys include knitwear,
tweeds, woollen, mohair and
Cashmere fabrics; Irish linen;
Waterford crystal glassware;
and handcrafted jewellery.
Main shopping areas include
pedestrianized **Grafton Street**
and **Dawson Street**, and
upmarket shopping malls like
Royal Hibernian Way, **St
Stephen's Green Shopping
Centre**, and **Powerscourt
Townhouse Centre**.

TOURS AND EXCURSIONS

Several companies offer sightseeing tours within Dublin City
and the most popular destina-
tions further afield.
Dublin City Tours: Dublin Bus
(*Bus Atha Cliath*), 59 Upper
O'Connell Street, Dublin 1, tel:

(01) 873-4222, daily tours on
open-topped buses, year-round
except winter Sundays.
C.I.E. Tours International, 35
Lower Abbey Street, Dublin 1,
tel: (01) 703-1888, offer daily
coach tours all around Ireland.
**Traditional Irish Musical Pub
Tour**. Two musicians play
instruments and lead you
around the music pubs. Meet at
St Oliver St John Gogarty pub,
Temple Bar at 19:30, nightly
May–Oct and Thu–Sat Nov–
Apr; tel: (01) 475-3313 to book.
**Jameson Dublin Literary Pub
Crawl** is a tour of Dublin's
best-known literary pubs with
an entourage of actors. Takes
place Easter to 31 October,
nightly 19:30; rest of the year,
Thursday–Saturday 19:30.
Starts at The Duke, Duke Street,
tel: (01) 670-5602 for bookings.
Coach Tours: Dublin Tourism
Centre, Suffolk Street, tel: (01)
605-7705. Tours to Glenda-
lough, Tara and further afield.
Limousine Tours: Tour Dublin
by limousine or helicopter with
guide, tel: (01) 872-3003.

USEFUL CONTACTS

Dublin Tourism Centre, offices
at Suffolk Street, tel: (01) 605
7705, also at Dun Laoghaire
Port Terminal Building and
Dublin International Airport.
Tourist Reservations, tel:
within Ireland 1 800 668 668,
from UK/France/Germany/
Sweden/Norway 00 800 668
668 66, from USA 011 800
668 668 66, from rest of the
world 00 353 669 2028.

3
Around Dublin

Bordered by County Meath, County Kildare and County Wicklow, County Dublin is watered by the **Liffey**, rising in Wicklow to flow through County Kildare and Dublin to the sea. The Royal Canal cuts County Dublin in two and leads westward, along the Meath–Kildare county line, while the Grand Canal runs from Dublin through Kildare to link the capital with Ireland's biggest waterway, the **Shannon**. No point in the county is more than 32km (20 miles), or about half an hour's drive, from the city centre. The **Dublin Mountains**, on the Wicklow border, are almost uninhabited.

COUNTY DUBLIN
Skerries

Skerries has a long, sandy beach and also three small islands – Shenick's Island, Colt Island and St Patrick's Island, with a **ruined church** said to have been built by the saint himself – just offshore. Midway between Skerries and the nearby village of Balbriggan, **Ardgillan Castle** is an 18th-century manor in landscaped grounds overlooking Drogheda Bay. Furnished in Victorian style with a **military history** theme, the ground-floor drawing room, morning room, dining room and library are open to visitors. The Heritage Centre is open from April–September daily 10:30–17:30; October–March daily 10:30–16:30; it is closed mid- to end December; guided tours take place from mid-May to mid-September, Saturday 15:30–16:30. The castle's park is open throughout the year from 10:00 until dusk.

DON'T MISS

*** Glendalough Visitor Centre: cradle of Irish Christianity, with 9th-century monastic buildings.
*** Newgrange Prehistoric Site: the most fascinating ancient archaeological site in Ireland.
*** Russborough House: palatial 18th-century manor house in the Palladian style.
** Hill of Tara: ancient standing stones mark seat of Ireland's High Kings.

Opposite: *The wild and picturesque mountain gorge of Glenmalure, in the Wicklow Mountains.*

Opposite: *The hills and glens of Wicklow are popular with walkers.*

Malahide ★★★

Malahide, once a seaside resort, is now a residential area. **Malahide Castle**, the home of the Talbot family from 1185 until the death of the last Lord Talbot in 1973, has a collection of **18th-century furniture**, displayed in two elegant drawing rooms. The 8ha (20-acre) **grounds** contain more than 5000 plant species and are at their brightest in early summer. Castle and the grounds are open Monday–Saturday 10:00–17:00, April–September Sunday 10:00–18:00, October–March Sunday 11:00–17:00.

Swords ★

Swords is one of the oldest Christian settlements in Ireland, founded in AD512 by St Colmcille, one of St Patrick's successors. Attractive 19th-century architecture includes **Swords Castle**, the fortified palace of the Archbishops of Dublin, who had estates here. The building of the castle began in the early 13th century, and it is now under extensive restoration. The adjacent 23m (75ft) **Round Tower** dates from the early Christian era.

Donabate ★★★

This tiny village, set on a magnificent peninsula, has one of the best beaches on the north Dublin coast. **Newbridge House**, set in 156ha (385 acres) of landscaped parkland, is a fine Georgian building. The **coach house** contains a State Coach dating from 1790 and an 18th-century charabanc built for the Duke of Manchester. Next to the mansion is an 8ha (20-acre) **working farm** stocked with native Irish farmyard breeds. Audiotape tours guide visitors through the house and grounds. Open April–September Tuesday–Saturday 10:00–17:00, Sundays 12:00–18:00; October–March Saturday–Sunday 12:00–17:00.

Lusk ★★

Lusk is a small farming town where in early Christian times the missionary St MacCullin founded a monastery. Lusk's small 19th-century **church** has quite an unusual square 16th-century belfry with four round towers, one of which dates from the 6th century. The belfry houses the **Lusk Heritage Centre**, with an exhibition on the region's many medieval churches. Open mid-June to September, daily 10:00–18:00.

The Wicklow Way ★★★

Among Ireland's finest walks, the Wicklow Way starts at **Marley Park**, south of Dublin, and runs through the Dublin and Wicklow Mountains to **Graiguemanagh** in County Kilkenny, approximately 130km (81 miles) to the south. Proper walking boots, wet-weather gear and a reliable map are essential.

COUNTY WICKLOW

County Wicklow, south of County Dublin, is wild and sparsely settled, though only a stone's throw from Dublin. Granite-bouldered glens and the barren slopes of the **Wicklow Mountains** are the characteristic scenery of the county.

Russborough House ★★★

Situated near Blessington, 3km (2 miles) southwest of the village on the N81 highway, is a palatial **manor house** in the Palladian style of the early 18th century. Russborough is the most splendid of Ireland's grand mansions. The magnificent rooms display fine stucco ceilings and are furnished with bronzes, silverware and china, tapestries and antique furniture. Russborough houses the **Beit Collection** of paintings, left by its last owner, Sir Alfred Beit. Open Easter–May and October Sundays and public holidays 10:00–17:00; May–September, daily 10:00–17:00.

Above: *The Round Tower at Glendalough, built to shelter Christian monks from Viking raiders.*
Opposite: *Statuary and mosaics among the lawns of Powerscourt Estate.*

Glendalough Visitor Centre ★★★

In this lovely green valley in the Wicklow Mountains **St Patrick's** disciple, **St Kevin**, founded a **monastery** in AD545 which managed to survive until the 16th century. The 33m (108 ft) **round tower** was used as a refuge from Viking raiders. Next to it stands the empty shell of the 9th-century **cathedral** and the 3.3m (11ft) **St Kevin's Cross**, dating from the mid-12th century. The Visitor Centre is open mid-March to mid-October, daily 09:30–18:00; mid-October to mid-March, daily 09:30–17:00.

Avondale House ★★

This late 18th-century mansion near Rathdrum, on the R752 road, was the home of **Charles Stewart Parnell**, the great 19th-century nationalist leader. Avondale has been refurbished, and an audiovisual presentation shows highlights of Parnell's life and political career. Open mid-March to October daily 11:00–18:00.

Powerscourt Estate and Gardens ★★

Powerscourt House burned down in the 1970s but its **gardens** are still a magnificent sight in spring and summer. Sloping to the lake, the grounds are planted with rare trees while behind them looms the steep outcrop of the **Great Sugar Loaf Mountain**. The centrepiece is Ireland's highest **waterfall**, boasting a 90m (295ft) drop.

COUNTY KILDARE

County Kildare, west of County Dublin, is a region of gentle landscapes, rich farmland and meandering rivers. **Maynooth**, on the N4 highway and straddling the Royal Canal, is the home of Ireland's oldest Catholic college.

St Patrick's College and Museum ★★

When it opened as a seminary in 1795, it was the first Catholic educational institution since the early 17th century. **Georgian** and **Victorian** buildings surround two quadrangles, built in 1795 and 1845 and over-looked by the steeple of the chapel, dating from 1875–77. The **museum** contains gadgets invented by college dons, including a primitive electrical battery and a horse-shoeing machine – a device that would surely have revolutionized transport had it not been for the simultaneous invention of the motor car. Open mid-June to mid-September, Tuesday and Thursday 14:00–16:00, Sunday 14:00–17:00.

COUNTY MEATH

County Meath, north of County Dublin, is a region of fertile, prosperous **farmland**. It was one of the cradles of early Celtic, pre-Christian Irish civilization, with some of the most outstanding relics of that heroic age. The **River Boyne** flows through the county, meeting the sea at Drogheda.

Drogheda ★★

Drogheda is one of Ireland's oldest settlements, with evidence of human habitation dating back at least two millennia. Parliamentary troops sacked it in 1649, slaughtering more than 1000 people in revenge for the massacre of Protestants during the 'Queen's Rising' of 1641. In the later conflict (1689–90) between the deposed King James II and William of Orange (William III), Drogheda was on the winning side. Among its few attractions is the

CROMWELL'S MASSACRES

In 1649 Oliver Cromwell, Lord Protector of England, arrived in Ireland with 20,000 soldiers to crush the Irish rising in favour of the **Royalist** side. At the siege of **Drogheda**, the Cromwellian troops massacred more than 1000 people, and at **Wexford** some 2000 inhabitants were slaughtered. Other strongholds in Royalist hands quickly surrendered for fear of further massacres. Cromwell's troops went on to burn castles, monasteries and cathedrals throughout the island.

Millmount Museum where exhibits include the sword and mace presented to the city by King William III in 1690. It is open in summer, daily 10:00–13:00 and 14:00–17:00; in winter, Wednesday, Saturday and Sunday 15:00–17:00.

Hill of Tara ★★

The seat of the **High Kings** at Tara was an important political and religious centre from the Stone Age well into the Christian era. A ring of 2m (6.5ft) **standing stones** is surrounded by rolling pasture. The gold **Tara Brooch**, found at the site, is on show in the National Museum. The interpretative centre at the foot of the hill is open May to mid-September, daily 09:30–18:00; mid-September to mid-October, daily 10:00–17:00.

Bru na Boinne (Newgrange, Dowth and Knowth Prehistoric Tombs) ★★★

Don't miss Ireland's most interesting archaeological site, off the N5 highway 1km (0.5 mile) east of Slane village. It comprises three **tomb clusters**, spread over several square kilometres on the banks of the Boyne, and is more than 2000 years old. Newgrange, the most fully explored and restored, is the most impressive. A **subterranean passage** leads into a great turf-covered **stone mound**, some 13.5m (44ft) high and 80m (262ft) in diameter. Within is a vast, 6m high (20ft) **domed chamber**, its walls ringed by mighty boulders carved into the complex curves and spirals of Celtic religious art. The neighbouring tombs at Knowth and Dowth have not yet been opened. This archaeological site is open all year round.

Below: *The Stone Age tomb clusters and standing stones at Newgrange, in the Boyne Valley.*

Around Dublin at a Glance

Bus Eireann (Irish Bus), 59 Upper O'Connell Street, Dublin 1, tel: (01) 836-6111, operates **bus services** from Dublin to all points in the surrounding counties. Depart from Busaras (Dublin Bus Station), Store Street, corner of Beresford Place and Amiens Street, 200m (220yd) south of Connolly Railway Station. Major international **car rental** companies have offices in central Dublin and at the airport: **Avis**, 35–9 Old Kilmainham, Dublin 8, tel: (01) 605-7500 (international reservations tel: (01) 677-6971 or book through travel agent before departure); **Hertz**, 151 South Circular Road, Dublin 8, tel: (01) 709-3060; **Murrays Europcar**, Baggot Street Bridge, Dublin 4, tel: (01) 614-2888. **DART** (Dublin Area Rapid Transit) and **Irish Rail Services** also connect Dublin with all coastal points including Drogheda and Dundalk in the north and Wicklow and Rathdrum in the south, and with Maynooth and Kildare to the west.

LUXURY
Fitzpatrick Castle Hotel, Killiney, County Dublin, tel: (01) 284-0700, fax: (01) 285-0207. Historic four-star in own landscaped gardens with view of Dublin Bay, 14km (9 miles) from the city centre.

Luttrellstown Castle Golf and Country Club, Castleknock, Dublin 15, tel: (01) 808-9988, fax: (01) 808-9989. Internationally renowned golf resort in 227ha (560 acres) of estate grounds, with a fine golf course which has hosted the Irish Open.
Finnstown Country House Hotel and Golf Course, Newcastle Road, Lucan, County Dublin, tel: (01) 628-0644, fax: (01) 628-1088. Set in 20ha (50 acres) of woodland with own nine-hole course.
Stand House Hotel and Country Club, Curragh Racecourse, County Kildare, tel: (045) 436-177, fax: (045) 436-180. De luxe hotel on Ireland's finest and oldest racing venue, The Curragh.

MID-RANGE
Monaghan's Harbour Hotel, Limerick Road, Naas, County Kildare, tel: (045) 879-145, fax: (045) 874-002. Comfortable family-run hotel. **Cullenmore Hotel**, Ashford, County Wicklow, tel: (0404) 40187, fax: (0404) 40471. Good quality hotel for touring the region, in foothills of the Wicklow Mountains, handy for Dublin.

BUDGET
Hotel Pierre, Victoria Terrace, Dun Laoghaire, County Dublin, tel: (01) 280-0291, fax: (01) 284-3332. Two-star hotel on Dublin Bay, ideal first stop when arriving by sea,

only two minutes from the ferry terminal and 15 minutes from central Dublin by DART. **Thomond House**, St Patrick's Road Upper, Wicklow Town, tel/fax: (0404) 67940. Excellent value guesthouse just outside Wicklow Town. **Grand Hotel**, Abbey Street, Wicklow Town, tel: (0404) 67337, fax: (0404) 69607. Slightly expensive but good value; 32 *en-suite* bedrooms.

LUXURY
The Old Schoolhouse Restaurant, Church Road, Swords, County Dublin, tel: (01) 840-2846, fax: (01) 840-5060. Unique atmosphere, good food, and attention to detail; noted for fish and game. Live music.

MID-RANGE
Mistral, 6 Harbour Road, Skerries, County Dublin, tel: (01) 849-1079, no fax. Steak, game and seafood *haute cuisine*, a bargain at lunchtime, moves into the luxury price bracket for dinner.

BUDGET
Lynham's, Laragh Inn, Glendalough, County Wicklow, tel: (0404) 45398, no fax. Pub of character and distinction serving generous portions of home cooking. **Murphy's**, 49 Main Street, Arklow, County Wicklow, tel: (0402) 32781, no fax. Family-run pub with restaurant.

4
The Southeast

Five counties – Waterford, Wexford, Carlow, Kilkenny and Tipperary – make up the southeast. Wexford, at the southeast tip of Ireland, and Waterford, midway along the south coast, have some fine **beaches** and pretty harbour towns, while inland Tipperary, Kilkenny and Carlow offer quiet farmland, rolling hills, and **scenic river valleys** dotted with market towns and quaint villages.

COUNTY WEXFORD

County Wexford faces both east, across the **Irish Sea**, and south, towards the Western Approaches and the **Atlantic**. Its strategic location has attracted invaders and settlers at least since the time of the Norsemen, and probably much earlier, and all have left their mark.

Wexford ★★

They say you can almost shake hands across Wexford's high street, and certainly this riverside town, founded by the **Vikings** in the 9th century, retains much of its old-time ambience. Wexford stands on a natural harbour, **Loch Garman**, at the mouth of the **River Slaney**.

The Norman **Selskar Abbey** was built in the 13th century, and stands on the site of an earlier Viking temple to Odin, chief of the Norse gods. Henry II did penance here in 1172 after the murder of Thomas à Becket at Canterbury Cathedral. It is now part of the **Westgate Heritage Centre**, comprising a 13th-century gate tower and part of the Norman walls. Open May–October, Monday–Friday 10:00–14:00, 14:30–17:00.

DON'T MISS

★★★ Irish National Heritage Park: 9000 years of history – lake dwellings, prehistoric and early medieval buildings.
★★★ Selskar Abbey and Westgate Heritage Centre: 13th-century Norman abbey.
★★★ Brownes Hill Dolmen: this toppled 4500-year-old monument is the largest of its kind in Europe.
★★★ Christ Church Cathedral: the only neoclassical Georgian Cathedral in Ireland.
★★★ Waterford Crystal Factory: master glassblowers and crystal cutters at work.

Opposite: *Hook Head lighthouse at County Wexford at low tide.*

Above: *Monument to the United Irishmen who rose in rebellion against Britain in 1798.*

IRISH COFFEE

Irish coffee is a 20th-century invention, and a good one – especially on a winter's day. It is simplicity itself to make: put a generous spoonful of **sugar** into a warmed, stemmed whiskey glass and pour in enough strong, hot black **coffee** to dissolve it. Stir thoroughly and add a good measure of **Irish whiskey**. To finish, slowly pour one tablespoon of cold **double cream** into the glass over the back of the spoon so that it floats on top of the whiskey-laced coffee.

Tintern Abbey was founded by William of Pembroke, Earl Marechal, in 1200, for the Cistercian order. It is currently under restoration, with limited access and variable opening hours. *See* Useful Contacts, page 73.

Irish National Heritage Park, Ferrycarrig ★★★

Just outside Wexford town, this is the southeast's top attraction, depicting 9000 years of **Irish history** with lake dwellings, prehistoric and early medieval buildings, a medieval castle, and a Viking shipyard recreated on a 14ha (35-acre) site near the Slaney River. Open daily 09:30–18:30 (all year round).

Johnstown Castle and National Museum of Agriculture and Rural Life ★★

Johnstown Castle, built in the 19th century for the **Earl of Desmond**, is situated about 7km (4 miles) southwest of Wexford. The **museum** is in the former estate farmyard in the grounds of this neo-Gothic castle. Although the castle is not open to the public, it is possible to visit the museum, highlights of which include a new exhibition on the Great Famine of 1845. The **grounds** also have pretty lakes and rare trees and shrubs.

Rosslare Ferryport ★

About 25km (15.5 miles) southeast of Wexford Town on the N25, on the east coast, Rosslare is an entry port for ferries to and from Wales. At **Yola Farmstead Folk Park**, 3km (2 miles) east of Rosslare Ferryport on the N25, stands **Tagoat**, a fascinating collection of traditional cottages, workshops, farm buildings and barns from the late 18th century. Open April–October daily 10:00–17:00.

John F Kennedy Arboretum ★

At New Ross, 30km (19 miles) west of Wexford Town on the N25, this 243ha (600-acre) arboretum has a collection comprising 4500 plant and tree species from every continent. It overlooks the birthplace of **Senator Joseph Kennedy**, father of US President John F Kennedy.

National 1798 Rebellion Centre ★★★

At Enniscorthy, some 24km (15 miles) north of Wexford Town on the N11, this centre uses multimedia to re-create the events of the 1798 revolution, culminating in the **Battle of Vinegar Hill**, fought here between rebel and Crown forces. Open Monday–Friday 09:30–17:00, Saturday–Sunday 11:00–17:00.

COUNTY CARLOW

Lying inland from Wexford and hemmed in by Kilkenny in the west and Laois, Kildare and Wicklow in the north, and known as the 'Celtic Centre of Ireland', Carlow has many **Celtic monuments** and historic sites. These include the notable dolmen at Browne's Hill and Irish 8th- and 9th-century **crosses** at villages such as Lorum, Nurney, Old Leighlin, St Mullins and Glebe Clonmore. In Carlow Town itself, **Carlow Cathedral**, completed in 1833, has a Gothic tower some 50m (164 ft) high. The cathedral is open daily.

About 4500 years old, **Browne's Hill Dolmen** is a toppled Stone-Age monument located approximately 8km (5 miles) southeast of Carlow Town on the N80. The largest capstone relic in Europe, the site marks the grave of an unknown Neolithic king. It is open daily during daylight hours.

Killeshin Church ★★

Built at Killeshin village, about 13km (8 miles) west of Carlow, during the reign of the Kings of Leinster in the 12th century, Killeshin church has a notable Irish-Romanesque doorway and 16th- and 18th-century additions. It stands on the site of a 6th-century monastery. The church is open daily during daylight hours.

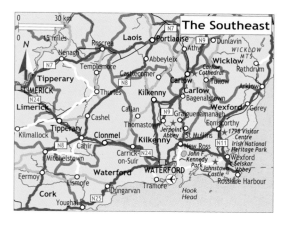

GOLF COURSES

Golf has become one of Ireland's biggest attractions, with over 350 superb golf courses around the country, many designed by some of the sport's biggest names. Golfers have the choice of challenging **links courses** – with the bonus of scenic beauty – and equally fine mature **parkland courses**. Many have hotels on site, some offering grand accommodation in former castles and country houses. Ireland hosted golf's top international tournament, the **Ryder Cup**, in 2005.

St Mullins Monastery Ruins and Gardens ★

This delightful collection of early monastic buildings and crosses is situated in pretty gardens in the valley of the River Barrow. The 7th-century monastery, of which the round tower still stands, was founded by St Moling (Mullin). Open May–September, Monday–Friday only.

Altamont Gardens ★

At Tullow, just off the N80, the complex embraces a formal 17th-century garden, 19th-century landscaped lake, woodland walks and the deep dramatic gorge of the River Slaney. Open daily 10:00–17:30.

COUNTY KILKENNY

County Kilkenny is the heart of the southeast. Sandwiched between Carlow and Tipperary and almost cut off from the sea by Waterford and Wexford, it has a tiny section of coastline at the head of the Barrow Estuary. Dubbed Ireland's 'medieval capital', **Kilkenny City** has the largest concentration of medieval churches and is also the best preserved Norman city in Ireland, with a section of the medieval town walls to be seen near **Black Friary Gate**, so called after the Dominican friars whose nearby **Black Abbey**, which was built in 1225, is still in use.

St Canice's Cathedral ★★★

The second longest cathedral in Ireland, St Canice's was built in 1285 and is decorated with **fine carvings** in wood and stone. Its 9th-century **round tower** can be ascended for a view of the city. Open April, May and September Monday–Saturday 10:00–17:00, Sunday 14:00–18:00; June–August Monday–Saturday 09:00–18:00, Sunday 14:00–18:00; October–March Monday–Saturday 10:00–13:00 and 14:00–16:00, Sunday 14:00–16:00.

Kilkenny Castle ★★★

Built in the 12th century and rebuilt in the 19th, and set among landscaped parkland, this was the seat of the **Butlers, Dukes of Ormonde** – one of Ireland's most powerful noble families. Restored in 1994, it houses a fine collection of **paintings, sculpture and furniture**. Open April–May daily 10:30–17:00; June–August daily 09:30–19:00; September daily 10:00–18:30; October–March, daily 10:30–12:45, 14:00–17:00.

CityScope Exhibition ★★

Located in the **Shee Almshouse** on Rose Street, this exhibition uses sound, light and scale models to re-create medieval Kilkenny. There is an interesting collection of **doll's houses**. Open May–September, Monday–Saturday 09:00–18:00; July–August, Monday–Saturday 09:00–21:00; October–April, Tuesday–Saturday 09:00–17:00.

Rothe House ★★★

Rothe House is a restored **Tudor merchant's home** with a collection of pictures and antiques, fine oak furniture and period costumes. It is owned by **Kilkenny Archaeological Society**, which also runs a family history research service for visitors. Open April–October; November–March Monday–Saturday 10:30–16:30.

Dunmore Cave ★★★

Near Ballyfoyle, 11km (7 miles) from Kilkenny on the N78, this cave with its weird **limestone chambers** and formations has been known since the 9th century and has a **visitor centre** with geological and historical displays. Access by guided tour only, open March–June, daily 10:00–17:00; June–September, daily 09:30–18:30; September–October, daily 10:00–17:00; November–February, Saturdays, Sundays and holidays 10:00–16:30.

Above: *Kilkenny Castle, built in the 12th century, stands guard over the river.* **Opposite:** *St Canice's Cathedral has the second longest aisle in Ireland.*

STONE WALLS

Typical of the Irish countryside in many regions are the dry stone walls, skilfully built **without mortar** and dividing the countryside into a patchwork of fields. The technique is ancient – there is evidence of its use **4000 years ago** – but most walls you see today date from the mid-19th century when, after the famine and the great emigration that followed, the land was redistributed and the older open system of farming abandoned. The tallest dry stone wall in the world is the one at the **Memorial Park** in **Islandbridge** in **Dublin**, built by masons brought from Connemara as a memorial to the Irish who died in World War I.

Above: *Christ Church Cathedral in Waterford is Ireland's only neoclassical Georgian cathedral.*

CELTS A MYTH?

The romantic myth of the ancient Celts – traditionally regarded as the ancestors of the modern Irish people – is no more than a 19th-century **invention**, according to some modern archaeologists and historians. In *The Atlantic Celts*, published in 1999, Iron-Age and Roman archaeologist **Simon Marsh** claims the 18th- and 19th-century 'Celtic revival', instead of reviving a Celtic tradition, in fact created the idea of a Celtic race to serve a range of cultural and political aspirations. There is **no real archaeological evidence** of separate Celtic 'race', archaeologists say.

Jerpoint Abbey ★★★

On the N9 road, 25km (15.5 miles) from Thomastown village, this beautiful **Cistercian abbey** was founded in the late 12th century and is noted for its **carved cloisters**. Open March–May and mid-September to October daily, 10:00–17:00.

Lory Meagher Homestead and Gaelic Athletic Association Museum (Brod Tullaroan) ★★

At Tullaroan, 16km (10 miles) west of Kilkenny, this 17th-century mansion has been restored in the period style of 1884. Formerly the home of Lory Meagher, a **hurling** star of the 1920s, it also houses an **exhibition** and **museum** of hurling and its heroes. Open March–June, Sun 14:00–17:30; June–August, Mon–Fri 10:00–17:30, Sun 14:00–17:30; September–November, Sun 14:00–17:30.

COUNTY WATERFORD

Waterford has a gentle, south-facing coastline with some fine **beaches**, several of which have received Blue Flag status for cleanliness, including Ardmore, Bunmahon, Clonea, and Councillors Strand. Inland are the glens and slopes of the **Comeragh Mountains**. With a warm summer climate, the county even has its own **vineyards**. The **Vikings** first landed at Waterford City, at the mouth of the River Suir, in AD852, to found the oldest continuously settled site in Ireland. Modern Waterford is an attractive mix of old and new, with modern shops, craft and design centres, traditional pubs and chic eating places.

Christ Church Cathedral ★★★

Earl **Strongbow**, Norman conqueror of Dublin, married **Aoife**, the daughter of Dermot McMurrough, Earl of Leinster, in the original 12th-century cathedral here, cementing a Norman-Irish dynasty. The present building dates from the 18th century and is the only neoclassical Georgian Cathedral in Ireland (or Britain). It features 'Let the Pillars Speak', an excellent 45-minute sound and light presentation. Open April–October, Monday–Saturday 10:00–17:00, Sunday 11:00–17:00.

Waterford Crystal Factory ★★★

Master glassblowers and crystal cutters work in this famed factory. The visitor centre has an **audiovisual show** and a **gallery** where Ireland's finest crystal is on sale. Factory tours March–October, daily 08:30–16:15; November–February, Monday–Friday 09:00–15:15.

Reginald's Tower ★★

The 12th-century tower guarding the harbour is Ireland's oldest civic building and it contains the **Civic and Maritime Museum** with marine exhibits and city regalia. Open Apr–May and Oct Sat–Sun 10:00–17:00; Jun–Sep Sat–Sun 09:30–18:30.

Curraghmore, Portlaw ★★★

A great stately home, Curraghmore has been the seat of the **Marquis of Waterford** and his dynasty since 1170. It has superb interior plasterwork and formal grounds graced by the 1754 **Shell Grotto** – the work of Catherine Power, Countess of Tyrone. Open Easter to mid-October, Thursdays and public holidays 14:00–17:00; guided tours January, May, June, Monday–Friday 09:00–13:00.

Tramore ★★

Tramore's **beach** is one of the most spectacular on the east coast, with golden sands stretching for miles. A holiday resort since Georgian times, it has modern facilities including a 20ha (50-acre) **amusement park** and marina.

An Rinn Irish Centre, Dungarvan ★

An Rinn centres around Colaista na Rinne, a cultural centre with year-round courses in Irish and a range of summer camp activities. Open June–August. For information, *see* Useful Contacts, page 73.

Ardmore Round Tower ★★★

St Declan, Bishop of Munster, brought Christianity some 16 years before St Patrick, in AD416. The 29m (95ft) Round Tower is a relic of one of the **oldest Christian settlements** in Western Europe. It is not open to the public.

IRISH NAMES

Many Irish people choose to christen their children with Irish names. Among the more common ones you may encounter are **Seamas**, the Irish equivalent of James; **Sean** (John); **Peadar** (Peter); **Proinsias** (Francis) and **Padraig** (Patrick). For girls, **Siobhain** is the Irish version of Joan and **Sinead** is the equivalent of Janet.

Below: *Waterford is famed for its fine crystal ware.*

SMOKING BAN

Smoking in pubs, restaurants and all indoor public spaces and public transport has been banned in the Republic of Ireland since March 2004. It is permissible to smoke outside, and many pubs now have outdoor tables – with patio heaters so they can be used even in cold weather.

Cappoquin ★

This quiet market town on the River Blackwater, in the Comeragh foothills, offers fine **trout fishing**. Cappoquin House Gardens are the attractive **formal gardens** of a Georgian manor house. Open April–July, Monday–Saturday 09:00–13:00.

It is also possible to taste local wine from 2000 vines growing in a lovely rural setting at **West Waterford Vineyards**. Open daily 10:00–20:00.

Lismore ★★★

A designated heritage town, Lismore has a fine cathedral, monastery and castle. The **Lismore Heritage Centre** in the former Lismore Court House is a multi-media show presenting the story of the city from the 7th century. Open April–May, September–October, Mon–Sat 09:30–17:30; June–August until 18:00; Sundays all year 12:00–17:30. **Lismore Castle** was built by King John in 1185, and is owned by the Duke of Devonshire. The gardens are open April–September, daily 13:45–16:45.

COUNTY TIPPERARY

Tipperary is noted for its lush **dairy pastures**, and has been dubbed the 'Golden Vale County'. But it has less pastoral landscapes too, in the **Slievefelim Mountains** and along the shores of **Lough Derg**, the southern-most of the chain of lakes along the **Shannon Water-way**. Many of the county's most striking sights and prettiest towns and villages are located on the banks of the **River Suir**, which eventually flows across the county line to meet the sea at Waterford.

Tipperary

Tipperary is quite a pleasant **small market town** overlooked by the Slievenamuck hills. Founded in the 12th century, its modern town plan and many of its buildings date from the 19th century. It's a good base for touring the region, but most of the county's historic sights lie well beyond the city limits.

Cashel ★★★

Cashel, the seat of the kings and bishops of Munster in medieval times, is one of Ireland's most significant **heritage sites**. The town is overlooked by the monolithic **Rock of Cashel**, a massive limestone outcrop which naturally attracted the attention of medieval builders. **Cormac**, King of Munster, built a **royal chapel** here in the 12th century and the striking complex of **medieval ruins** includes the cathedral, round tower, Romanesque chapel and restored choral hall. Attractions include multilingual **audiovisual show**, 'Strongholds of the Faith'. Open daily, mid-June to mid-September 09:00–19:30; mid-September to mid-March 09:00–16:30.

Next to the Rock, **Brú Ború** has an **information centre** and theatre with its own resident troupe of Irish singers and musicians, craft centre, restaurant and genealogy centre. Centre open May–September, daily 09:00–18:00; performances June–September, Tuesday–Saturday 21:00; craft shop open daily 09:00–18:00 year-round.

In Cashel town centre, **Cashel Folk Village** includes reconstructed traditional thatched houses, shops, workshops and forge. Open daily March–April 10:00–18:00; May–October 09:30–19:30. Nearby, the **Cashel Heritage Centre** features a large-scale model of the mid-17th-century town, with royal relics and heirlooms of pre-Norman Ireland. Open March–August daily 09:30–17:30; November–February, Monday–Friday 09:30–17:30.

Above: *The Rock of Cashel is crowned by medieval ruins.*
Opposite: *Ireland has some world-class golf courses, like this one at Lismore, and hosts a number of national and international tournaments.*

SPANISH ARMADA

Decimated by Sir Francis Drake's fleet as they straggled through the English Channel in 1588 in their abortive attempt to invade England, the galleons of the Spanish Armada were swept by gales through the North Sea and attempted to make their way home by way of the Scottish Hebrides and Ireland, where several of them came to grief. The Duqesa Santa Ana ran aground at Loughros More Bay, on the Donegal coast, and the Girona, which picked up the survivors, went down off Antrim with the loss of more than 1000 lives.

Above: *Cahir Castle stands on a small island in the River Suir.*

Cahir Castle ★★

Standing on an islet in the Suir, this is one of the finest and best preserved of medieval strongholds. Highlights include 'Partly Hidden, Partly Revealed', an **audiovisual show** featuring Tipperary's main sites. Open mid-March to mid-June, daily 09:30–17:30; mid-June to mid-September, daily 09:00–19:30; mid-September to mid-October, daily 09:30–17:30; mid-October to mid-March, daily 09:30–16:30.

A pleasant 2km (1-mile) walk along the river south from Cahir Castle Park, **Swiss Cottage**, the delightful thatched country home of **Richard Butler**, first Earl Glengall, was designed in the early 19th century by John Nash and is elegantly decorated within in Regency style. Open for guided tours only, March and October–November, Tuesday–Sunday 10:00–13:00, 14:00–16:30; April 10:00–13:00, 14:00–18:00; May–September, daily 10:00–18:00.

Carrick-on-Suir ★★

On the banks of the Suir, between the Slievenamon and Comeragh hills, the main attraction in town is **Ormond Castle**. Built for the 10th Earl of Ormond in the mid-16th century, this is said to be the **finest Elizabethan mansion** in Ireland. It incorporates two earlier 15th-century defensive towers, and its fine reception rooms have superb stucco decorations including plaster portraits of the Ormonds. Open (guided tours only) June to September, daily 10:00–17:00, October–March daily 10:00–16:00.

Carrick-on-Suir Heritage Centre is a former Protestant church, restored as a heritage centre within the 17th-century **graveyard**. It has a display of local photographs and the 17th-century Duke of Ormond Church Silver. Open daily 09:30–18:30 (not open in winter).

The Southeast at a Glance

BEST TIMES TO VISIT

The region has a gentle climate and can be visited year-round but as the lush pasture lands show, winter rainfall is heavy and rain is a possibility year-round. The best time to visit is **June–September**, though sights, roads and beaches are at their busiest in July and August.

GETTING THERE

By Air: Waterford Regional Airport has flights from several UK airports.
By Sea: Ferries to Rosslare from Roscoff and Cherbourg in France, Pembroke in Wales.
By Road: The main N11 east-coast highway connects Wexford with Dublin, while the N25 south-coast highway runs between Wexford and Waterford and on to Cork. The N9 connects Waterford with Kilkenny, Carlow and Dublin. Bus services connect all major towns with Dublin.
By Rail: Trains connect Wexford with Dublin and run between Wexford, Waterford, Carrick, Cahir, Tipperary and Limerick, with connections to Cork. There are services between Waterford and Dublin.

GETTING AROUND

Frequent daily **buses** connect all towns in the area. Three **rail** lines traverse the region (see above), with several services daily. For Irish Rail and Bus Eireann information, tel: (051) 73401.

WHERE TO STAY

LUXURY
Marlfield House, Gorey, County Wexford, tel: (055) 21124, fax: (055) 21572. Four-star renovated former home of Earls of Courtown, with 13 bedrooms, award-winning restaurants and 13.5ha (33 acres) of grounds.

MID-RANGE
Bridge Hotel, 1 The Quay, Waterford, tel: (051) 877-222, fax: (051) 877-229. Family-run city-centre hotel with harbour views and three fine restaurants.
White's Hotel, Abbey Street, Wexford, tel: (053) 22311, fax: (053) 45000. Efficient, recently modernized city-centre hotel.
Old Rectory Hotel, Rosbercon, New Ross, County Wexford, tel: (051) 421-719, fax: (051) 422-971. All rooms *en suite*, good restaurant, gardens overlooking River Barrow.

BUDGET
Coach House, Butlerstown Castle, Butlerstown, Cork Road, Waterford, tel: (051) 384-656, fax: (051) 384-751, cheap and convenient.
Faythe Guest House, Swan View, Wexford Town, tel: (053) 22249, fax: (053) 21680, good value for money.
Legends Guesthouse and Restaurant, The Kiln, Cashel, County Tipperary, tel: (062) 61292, fax: (062) 62876, comfortable rooms, good food.

WHERE TO EAT

LUXURY
Bells Restaurant, Granville Hotel, Meagher Quay, Waterford, tel: (051) 855-111. French steak and seafood restaurant.

MID-RANGE
The Olde Stand, 45 Michael Street, Waterford, tel: (051) 879-488. Affordable steak and seafood restaurant.

BUDGET
Loughmans Restaurant, George's Court, Barrowstand Street, Waterford, tel: (051) 878-704. Café-restaurant, Irish, continental, vegetarian.

USEFUL CONTACTS

Tintern Abbey in Wexford, tel: (01) 661-3111.
An Rinn Irish Centre in Dungarvan, tel: (058) 46128.
South East Tourism Information Offices, linked to the computerized **Gulliver** information and reservation service, at the following addresses:
Kilkenny
Shee Alms House, Rose Inn St, Kilkenny, tel: (056) 775-1500, fax: (056) 776-3955.
Rosslare
Terminal Building, Rosslare Harbour, tel: (053) 33622, fax: (053) 33421.
Waterford
41 The Quay, Waterford, tel: (051) 875-823, fax: (051) 876-720.
Wexford
Crescent Quay, Wexford, tel: (053) 23111, fax: (053) 41743.

5
The Southwest

Ireland's southwest comprises four counties, including among them some of the most evocative names in Irish history, song and legend. Cork, Kerry, Clare and Limerick have widely varying land- and seascapes, ranging from the south-facing **beaches** of the Cork coast to the **windswept cliffs** and hillsides of the more rugged Atlantic coast.

CORK CITY

Ireland's third city, Cork is at once a place steeped in history and a forward-looking modern community. Situated on an estuary opening onto the Atlantic, it has a strong maritime identity and the **Royal Cork Yacht Club** is one of the world's oldest.

St Finbarr's Cathedral ★

Completed in 1870, the cathedral is noted for its stained glass, carvings, mosaics and more than 1200 sculptures. Open 1 April to 30 September, Monday–Saturday 10:00–17:30; 1 October to 31 March, Monday–Saturday 10:00–12:45, 14:00–17:00.

St Anne's Shandon Church and Steeple ★

Built in 1722, this is one of Cork's most prominent landmarks, with its salmon-shaped weather vane and 36m (120ft) steeple housing the famous **Shandon Bells**, which visitors are allowed to ring. Open 1 April to 30 September, Monday–Saturday 09:30–17:30; 1 October to 31 March, Monday–Saturday 10:00–16:00.

DON'T MISS

★★ Cork City Gaol: recreates the grim atmosphere of its past, with cells furnished with lifesize figures.
★★★ Queenstown Story: this heritage centre tells the story of the millions of emigrants who passed through the port of Cork.
★★★ Blarney Castle Estate: the most famous visitor attraction in Ireland, with the Blarney Stone set into the castle wall.
★★ Barryscourt Castle: 12th–15th-century tower house.

Opposite: *Cork's streets are lined with attractive old buildings.*

Cork City Gaol ★★

The 19th-century building recreates the grim atmosphere of its past, with cells furnished with lifesize figures representing every era from pre-Famine Ireland to the 1920s. A **sound and image show** recounts the social history of the city. Open Mar–Oct daily 09:30–17:00, Nov–Feb 10:00–16:00.

Beamish and Crawford Brewery ★★

Founded in 1792, the Beamish and Crawford Brewery on South Main Street is the **oldest in Ireland**, with part of the original building still forming part of the modern building. Open Tuesday and Thursday for tours and tastings, 10:30 and 12:00; must be booked ahead.

Cobh, The Queenstown Story ★★★

Cobh, known under British rule as Queenstown, is the **port district** of Cork. This **heritage centre** tells the story of the millions of emigrants who passed through it in the 19th and 20th centuries; the convicts who were transported to the Australian penal colonies; and great ocean liners such as the *Lusitania*, torpedoed off Cork in 1917, and the ill-fated *Titanic*, which made its last port of call here. Open May–Oct daily 09:30–18:00, Nov–Apr 09:30–17:00.

AROUND CORK

Cork is a county of steep hillsides and river valleys, sea cliffs and deeply indented coastline where the Atlantic meets the Irish Sea. **Natural harbours** like Kinsale make the region a favourite with modern yachtsmen no less than ancient invaders from the Vikings to the Spaniards.

Cork

Kinsale

One of the most attractive coastal villages in Ireland, Kinsale stands on a perfect natural harbour which is a favourite with yacht sailors. It was the scene of abortive Spanish and French landings in support of **Irish risings** against the English in the 16th and 17th centuries.

Built in the early 1680s, the star-shaped **Charles Fort**, commanding the entrance to Kinsale's natural harbour just south of the village, is a classic example of military architecture of the time. Held by Jacobite forces in the Orange-Jacobite struggle of 1688–91, it was besieged and taken by the Duke of Marlborough for King William and remained in use until 1922, when it was partially destroyed during the Civil War. The ruins of **James Fort**, an earlier structure built in 1602 for King James VI and I, stand on the opposite side of the estuary. Open mid-Apr to mid-Jun and mid-Sep to mid-Oct Sat–Mon 09:00–17:00; mid-Jun to mid-Sep daily 09:00–18:00.

Now housing an international wine museum, **Desmond Castle** in the centre of the village was originally a custom house for the Earl of Desmond, built around 1500, and was subsequently a prison and a workhouse. Open daily 10:00–18:00, closed Mondays in April.

Blarney Castle Estate ★★★

Perhaps the most famous visitor attraction in Ireland, the **Blarney Stone** is set into the castle wall. Kissing it is said to confer the gift of **eloquence**, and much of the year there is a long queue of visitors waiting to test its powers. The castle is one of Ireland's oldest, with walls that are up to 5.5m (18ft) thick, and belonged to the McCarthy lords of Muskerry. Open May and Sep Mon–Sat 09:00–18:30, Sun 09:30–17:30, Jun–Aug Mon–Sat 09:00–19:00, Sun 09:30–17:30, Oct–Apr 09:30 until dusk.

Above: *Kissing the Blarney Stone is supposed to confer the gift of the gab.*

THE *LUSITANIA*

It was some 24km (15 miles) off the **Head of Kinsale**, south of Cork, that the ill-fated British liner *Lusitania* was torpedoed by a **German U-boat** in 1915, resulting in the deaths of 1198 passengers and seamen. Over 100 of the passengers were American, which caused a great fuss, and helped to swing Americans in favour of intervention in **World War I** two years later.

Above: *The steep hillsides and moors of Gougane Barra National Park.*

MICHAEL COLLINS

Michael Collins (1890–1922) was born near **Clonakilty**, County Cork, in 1890. In 1916 he was among the defenders of the GPO during the **Easter Rising**. With Eamon de Valera and Arthur Griffith he was a leader of the **Republican** movement, and the military genius behind the war of ambush and assassination against the British from 1919–21. In 1921, he and Griffith led the Irish delegation in the treaty negotiations which created the **Free State** and led to civil war. In August 1922 he was killed by IRA fighters in West Cork. His **birthplace** is signposted on the N71 highway west of Clonakilty village. The spot where he was ambushed and killed at Beal na Blath, in West Cork, is also signposted and marked by a stone **memorial**.

Jameson Heritage Centre – Old Midleton Distillery, Midleton ★★

Visitors may go on a one-hour tour of the well-restored 18th-century distillery complex, with the largest **copper pot** still in existence (145,600 litres or 32,000 gallons), as well as a working water-wheel and a multilingual audiovisual presentation. The distillery is open Mar–Oct, daily 09:00–17:00; Nov–Feb three tours daily, 11:30, 14:30 and 16:00.

Barryscourt Castle, Carrigtwohill ★★

This fine 15th-century tower house, with three towers dating from as early as the 12th century, was the seat of the **Barry family** until the 17th century. The ground floor now houses a local **museum**. Open Jun–Sep daily 10:00–18:00.

Gougane Barra National Park ★★

Near Ballingeary, and a favourite spot for trout fishers and walkers, the park is an area of steep hillsides around **Lake Lee**, with a tiny island which was the hermitage retreat of **St Finbarr**, patron saint and founder of Cork City. Open all year.

Bantry

Bantry Bay is a deep natural harbour that has served as a British and Irish naval and fishing base and now shelters Ireland's largest **oil tanker terminal**. The 1796 **Bantry French Armada Centre** tells the story of the French frigate *Surveillante*, which was scuttled in the Bay during the abortive French invasion attempt of 1796 and rediscovered and declared a national monument in 1985. The centrepiece of the exhibition is a 1:6 scale **model of the ship**. Open Apr–Oct, daily 10:00–18:00.

COUNTY KERRY

For many visitors, the wild Atlantic seascapes of the Kerry coast are what Ireland is all about, and the often rugged scenery of the county is in sharp contrast to the gentler, more pastoral landscapes of its neighbours to the east. The lovely **Dingle Peninsula**, pointing deep into the Atlantic surf, is the westernmost point of Europe. Inhospitable compared to other parts of the island, Kerry has always been more thinly populated and thus has fewer major historic sights than neighbouring Cork, but makes up for this with striking **natural beauty** and several excellent new purpose-built **visitor attractions**.

Killarney

Beautifully located among scenic lakes and mountains, Killarney is a charming small town and an ideal base for exploring the southwest of Ireland. Just off the main Killarney-Kenmare road, about 2.5km (1.5 miles) from the town centre, is the 14th-century **Ross Castle**. Open daily 09:00–17:00.

Muckross House, Gardens and Traditional Farms at Muckross Village is a Victorian mansion with its own craft workshops, nature trails and also a craft shop. Open daily 09:00–17:30.

Kenmare

Built to a distinctive X-pattern plan in the 18th century by the Lansdowne family, the local landowners, Kenmare is famed for its **lace making**. Just outside town stand the remains of a 4000-year-old **stone circle**.

Next to the Kenmare Tourist Office, **Kenmare Heritage Centre** features Kenmare, its history and its crafts with multilingual Sound Tour headsets, a gift shop and a heritage trail map. It is open Apr–Sep daily 09:00–17:30, Sun 09:00–13:00.

DON'T DROP LITTER

Don't be tempted to drop your litter in the street or by the road. In a draconian bid to curb Ireland's growing garbage problem, on-the-spot **fines for littering** were introduced in 1998, and wardens and police officers can now fine you 32 euros on the spot for littering, and up to a maximum fine of 1,900 euros if you are taken to court.

Below: *Kerry has a dramatic Atlantic coastline.*

Crag Cave ★★

Signposted from Castleisland Village on the N21 highway and opened up only in 1983, this is one of Ireland's **longest cave systems**, with almost 4km (2.5 miles) of limestone tunnels and caverns surveyed, 350m (383yd) of which are open to the public, with easily accessible paths and coloured lighting systems illuminating the dramatic spires and stalactites. Open March–October, daily 10:00–18:00; June–August, daily 10:00–18:30.

The Skellig Experience ★★★

The barren, barely habitable **Skellig Rocks** were a refuge for early Christian monks, who left unique, **beehive-like monastery buildings**. The Skellig Experience, at Valentia Island, opposite Portmagee Village, tells the tale of the 6th-century monks and 19th-century lighthousemen who lived here and of the unique bird life and sea life of the Skelligs and the surrounding waters. Open April–November, daily 10:00–18:00.

Kerry the Kingdom, Aske Memorial Hall, Tralee ★★

Excellent **indoor multimedia show** brings urban Ireland in the Middle Ages to life with modern sound and image systems and archaeological treasures. Commentaries are in eight languages. Located in Denny Street, it is open March–December daily 09:00–17:00.

Dingle Oceanworld Aquarium ★★

Overlooking Dingle Harbour, the aquarium has a walk-through tunnel tank and a shark tank, interactive screens telling the story of **St Brendan the Navigator** (and the recreation of his legendary voyage by adventurer Tim Severin), and finds from the **Spanish Armada**, some of whose storm-tossed galleons went down in these waters. Open daily 10:00–17:00 (year round).

COUNTY LIMERICK
Limerick City ★★

Capital not only of Limerick County but also of the surrounding Shannon Region, Limerick is a vibrant city that mixes old and new. Designated as Ireland's 'Music Centre of Excellence', the city is the home of the **Irish Chamber Orchestra** and the venue for the **Summerfest** of classical music and the **Paddy Music Expo** of jazz, blues, folk and rock in May. The town's top attractions include **King John's Castle**, one of Ireland's most impressive fortresses, which stands on the Shannon, in the heart of Limerick's medieval town centre. New exhibitions and a multimedia show are under development; *see* Useful Contacts, page 85. **Castle Lane** is the 18th- and 19th-century Irish townscape next to the Castle, housing the **Limerick Civic Museum** and the new **Castle Lane Tavern**, an entertainment, music and dance centre under development. For opening hours, *see* Useful Contacts, page 85.

Also worth visiting in Limerick is the **Custom House and Limerick Hunt Museum**, a superb collection of 2000 works of art, religious pieces and antiquities in a Georgian building. Open Mon–Sat 09:00–17:00, Sun 14:00–17:00.

Adare ★★★

Claimed to be Ireland's prettiest village, Adare nestles in the wooded valley of the **River Maigue**. Adare owes its pretty thatched cottages to the local landowners, the **Earls of Dunraven**, who ensured their survival in the 19th century, when elsewhere in Ireland thatch was being replaced by slate.

Left: *Thatched cottage at Adare, said to be the prettiest village in Ireland.* **Opposite:** *The Gallarus Oratory on the Dingle Peninsula, home of a famous hermit.*

THE BARD OF THOMOND

The works of Limerick's 19th-century poet, the 'Bard of Thomond', **Michael Hogan** (d.1899), have been reprinted for modern readers thanks to the Bard's great great grandsons, Limerick-born Noel and Michael Hogan of the Irish band **The Cranberries**, who financed the reissue of the poet's *Lays and Legends of Thomond* in 1999, a century after his death. Limerick Corporation also honoured the poet by erecting a **bronze statue** at King John's Castle.

Lough Gur ★★

Approximately 6km (3.5 miles) from Limerick City, the Lough Gur Interpretative Centre recreates a **Neolithic village** of 5000 years ago. Open mid-May to end Sep, daily 10:00–18:00.

COUNTY CLARE

Golden Atlantic **beaches**, peaceful countryside, fields, farmland and forest are among the attractions of County Clare. The high point is one of Europe's most extraordinary **pocket wildernesses**, the Burren.

Above: *This Stone-Age dolmen stands amid the barren limestone landscape of the Burren.*

Ennis

Clare's county town on the **River Fergus** dates from 1240, when the local lord, Donnachadh Cairbreach O'Brien, invited the Franciscan order to establish a **Friary**, the roofless gables, tower and churchyard of which may still be seen. The 15th-century **MacMahon tomb**, in the churchyard, is noted for its carvings of the Passion. Open Apr–May and Sep–Oct Tue–Sun 10:00–17:00, Jun–Aug daily 10:00–18:00.

The Southwest

Map legend and place names:
Inishmore, Inisheer, Aran Islands, Cliffs of Moher, Hags Head, Donegal Point, Loop Head, Kerry Head, Sybil Point, Tralee Bay, Dingle, Dingle Bay, Valentia Island, Bolus Head, Bear Island, Dunmanus Bay, Mizen Head, Clear Island, Galley Head, Old Head of Kinsale, Summer Ferries, Loughrea, Gort, Ennistyman, Ennis, Clare, Lough Derg, Nenagh, Tipperary, LIMERICK, Shannon, Kilrush, Rathkeale, Lough Gur, Limerick, Listowel, Newcastle West, Charleville, Tralee, Kerry, Castleisland, Mitchelstown, Killorglin, Cork, Killarney, Mallow, Fermoy, Lough Leane, Millstreet, Cahersiveen, Killarney National Park, Blarney, Midleton, Kenmare, Macroom, CORK, Cloyne, Gougane Barra National Park, Cobh, Kenmare River, Bantry Bay, Bantry, Bandon, Kinsale, Skibbereen, Clonakilty, Ferry to Wales

0 30 km
0 15 miles
N
N18, N7, N24, N21, N20, N22, N8, N25

Quin Abbey ★★

At Quin, a small village about 12km (7.5 miles) southeast of Ennis, the grey stone walls and tower of the 14th-century Abbey stand on site of a 13th-century castle built by the Norman lord, **Richard de Clare**. The cloisters date from 1402. Open daily, daylight hours.

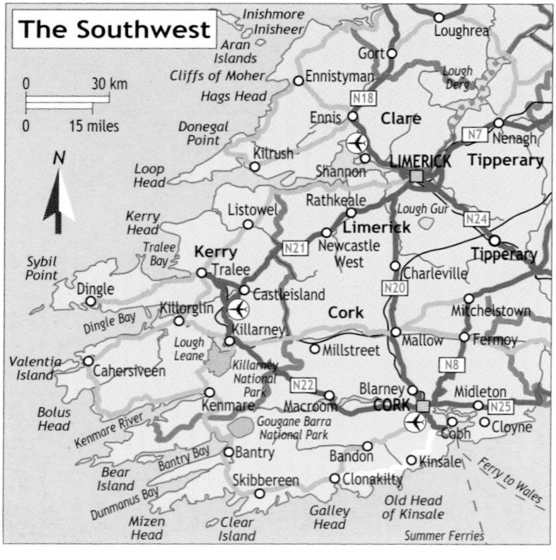

Dysert O'Dea Castle and Clare Heritage Centre ★★

At Dysert O'Dea, 8km (5 miles) north of Ennis, the O'Dea clan's 15th-century stronghold stands in fields among 25 other **historic monuments**, including two Romanesque churches, a 12th-century High Cross, two Celtic forts and a holy well. Open May–September, daily 10:00–18:00.

The Burren ★★★

Caves and natural limestone pavements ('clints') split by fissures ('grykes') are features of this landscape, dotted with Stone-Age **tombs** and stone **forts** called 'cahers'. At 160km² (62 sq miles), the Burren is also famous for its **plants**. Burren Display Centre, Kilfenora, open daily March–May and September–October, 10:00–17:00; June–August, daily 09:30–19:00.

Ailwee Cave ★★

These spectacular **limestone formations** in water-carved caverns which extend for some 600m (656yd) into the hillside were opened up only in 1944. Open daily 10:00 until dusk (year round).

Below: *The giant natural ramparts of the Cliffs of Moher, on the Clare coast.*

Cliffs of Moher and O'Brien's Tower ★★★

Just north of Lahinch, these giant **natural ramparts** stand 215m (705ft) above the Atlantic and stretch 8km (5 miles) along the West Clare coast. **O'Brien's Tower**, built in the 19th century, stands on the highest point. Visitors' centre open May–June, daily 09:00–18:30; July–August, daily 09:00–21:00; September–April, daily 09:30–18:00. Tower open May–June, daily 09:30–18:00; July–August, daily 09:30–20:30; September–April, daily 10:00–17:30.

Lough Derg ★★★

A 12,950ha (32,000-acre) expanse of calm, clear water fed by the Shannon and stretching between **Portumna** at its north end and **Ballina** in the south, Lough Derg lies on the county border between Clare and Tipperary, with its northern part stretching into Galway. The lough is popular in summer for sailing, fishing, bird-watching and motor-boating.

The Southwest at a Glance

Like the other southern counties, Cork and Kerry can be visited year-round, but if you want to make the most of the region's splendid outdoor pursuits, which include walking, fishing, cycling, surfing and windsurfing or just beachcombing, the wet and windy winter months, November to March, are best avoided. **July** and **August** are peak tourist season. Many smaller hotels and restaurants, and many tourist attractions, are closed from November to March.

By Air: Scheduled flights to Limerick, Kerry and Cork International from Dublin, Belfast, London, Manchester, Glasgow and several European airports, and scheduled and charter flights to Shannon International Airport from Dublin, Belfast, London, the USA and Canada.
By Sea: There are regular ferries from Swansea by Swansea-Cork Ferries.
By Road: The main N22 highway connects Cork with Killarney and Tralee. The N25 connects Cork with Waterford and points east, the N20 runs north-south between Cork and Limerick, while the N21 runs northeast from Killarney to Limerick.
By Rail: Trains run between Cork and Limerick via Limerick Junction, and also between Cork, Killarney and Tralee.

Cork has an efficient local **bus** service. Elsewhere within the region, Bus Eireann services connect towns and villages.

Most accommodation is in two- and three-star hotels and in bed and breakfast and farmhouse accommodation, with a sprinkling of comfortable country house hotels.

Counties Cork and Kerry
LUXURY
Aherne's, 163 North Main Street, Youghal, County Cork, tel: (024) 92424, fax: (024) 93633, e-mail: ahe@iol.ie Comfortable, traditional family-run hotel with award-winning seafood restaurant.
Assolas Country House, Kanturk, County Cork, tel: (029) 50015, fax: (029) 50795, e-mail: assolas@tinet.ie Seven-bedroom country house hotel with award-winning gardens. Open 25 March to 1 November.
Blue Haven Hotel, Pearse Street, Kinsale, County Cork, tel: (021) 477-2209, fax: (021) 774-268, e-mail: info@ bluehavenkinsale.com Small, cosy hotel in a period building in the historic heart of Kinsale.
Park Hotel Kenmare, Kenmare, County Kerry, tel: (064) 41200, fax: (064) 41402, e-mail: info@parkkenmare.com Five-star country house hotel with 4.5ha (11-acre) grounds and 18-hole golf course.

MID-RANGE
Jury's Inn Cork, Anderson's Quay, Cork City, County Cork, tel: (021) 494-3000, fax: (021) 427-6144. Comfortable, conveniently located three-star hotel.
Doyle's Seafood Bar and Townhouse, John Street, Dingle, County Kerry, tel: (021) 915-1174, fax: (021) 915-1816. Cosy, traditional four-star guesthouse with eight rooms and restaurant noted for lobster. Open mid-March to mid-November.

BUDGET
Wander Inn, Henry Street, Kenmare, County Kerry, tel: (064) 41038, fax: (064) 41408. Open year-round.
Foley's Shamrock, Henry Street, Kenmare, County Kerry, tel: (064) 42162, fax: (064) 41799. Three-star guesthouse, central and affordable.

County Clare
LUXURY
Gregans Castle, Ballyvaughan, County Clare, tel: (065) 077-7005, fax: (065) 077-7111, e-mail: stay@ gregans.ie On the edge of the Burren with Galway Bay views, four-star country house hotel.

MID-RANGE
Auburn Lodge Hotel, Galway Road, Ennis, County Clare, tel: (065) 682-1247, fax: (065) 682-1202. Conveniently located three-star hotel.

The Southwest at a Glance

BUDGET
Cill Eoin Guesthouse,
Kildysert Cross, Ennis,
County Clare, tel: (065) 684-1668, fax: (065) 682-0224.
Three-star guesthouse,
comfortable, friendly and
affordable.

County Limerick
LUXURY
Limerick Strand Hotel,
Ennis Road, Limerick City,
tel: (061) 453-033, fax: (061)
453-307. A contemporary,
elegant hotel right in the heart
of the city, with on-site
indoor pool, steam room
and stylish restaurant.
Castletroy Park Hotel,
Castletroy, County Limerick,
tel: (061) 335-566, fax: (061)
311-117. Comfortable five-star
in suburb of Limerick City.

MID-RANGE
Dunraven Arms Hotel,
Adare, County Limerick,
tel: (061) 396-633, fax: (061)
396-541. This charming hotel,
decorated with antiques, has
been in operation since 1792.
There's also an on-site pool.

BUDGET
Clon Ross, 85 Lower
Glanmire Road, Cork City,
County Cork, tel: (021) 502-602, no fax. Very affordable
two-star guesthouse.
Hanratty's Hotel, Glentworth
Street, Limerick, County
Limerick, tel: (061) 41099,
fax: (061) 411-077.
Affordable small hotel.

WHERE TO EAT

LUXURY
Aherne's, 163 North Main
Street, Youghal, County Cork,
tel: (024) 92424, fax: (024)
93633, e-mail: ahe@iol.ie
Award-winning seafood
restaurant.
**O'Connor's Seafood
Restaurant**, The Square,
Bantry, County Cork, tel:
(027) 50221, fax: (027)
50011. Speciality seafood,
steak and game restaurant.
Man Friday, Scilly, Kinsale,
County Cork, tel: (021) 477-2260, fax: (021) 477-2262.
Gourmet fish restaurant.
Café Indigo, The Square,
Kenmare, County Kerry.
Stylish café-restaurant serving
internationally inspired
cuisine, offers a light late-night menu from 22:30.

MID-RANGE
Finians, 75 Main Street,
Midleton, County Cork, tel:
(021) 463-1878, fax: (021)
463-2382. Wine bar with
seafood, steak and duck
on menu.
Fenton's, Green Street,
Dingle, County Kerry, tel:
(066) 51209, fax: (066)
51385. Pretty restaurant
serving tasty local produce,
also offers four-star guest-house accommodation.
**Brannagans Restaurant and
Bar**, Mill Road, Ennis,
County Clare, tel: (065)
20211, fax: (065) 41153.
Commendable Irish pub-restaurant.

BUDGET
The Brazenhead,
102 O'Connell Street,
Limerick, tel: (061) 417-412,
fax: (061) 417-922.
Restaurant-bar and nightclub
in the city centre.

TOURS AND EXCURSIONS
Shannon cruising:
Motor river cruisers can be
hired from R&B Marine
Services, Killaloe, County
Clare, tel: (061) 375-011, and
from Shannon Castle Line,
tel: (061) 927-042.

USEFUL CONTACTS

Cork
Cork Kerry Tourism,
Aras Failte, Grand Parade,
Cork, tel: (021) 425-5100,
fax: (021) 425-5199.
Killarney
Cork Kerry Tourism, Beech
Street, Killarney, tel: (064)
31633, fax: (064) 34506.
Tralee
**Shannon Tourism
Development**,
Town Centre, Tralee,
tel: (066) 21288,
fax: (061) 361-555.
Limerick
**Shannon Tourism
Development**, Arthur's
Quay, Limerick City,
tel: (061) 338-177,
fax: (061) 317-939.
For information about new
exhibitions in Limerick,
tel: (061) 361-511.
For opening hours of **Castle
Lane**, tel: (1800) 269-811
toll free.

6
The West

The wild, sometimes brooding landscapes of Ireland's far western region, where the rugged mountain slopes meet a magnificent Atlantic coastline consisting of wide bays, sweeping stretches of sandy beach and lovely, near-deserted islands, is never to be forgotten. Inland from the Atlantic coasts of Galway and Mayo lie the much gentler pastoral landscapes and a beautifully scenic **lake district**. The far west is also very closely associated with several of the great figures of Ireland's literary and cultural renaissance, most notably W B Yeats, Oliver St John Gogarty, J M Synge and also Yeats's patron, Lady Gregory.

The **Gaeltacht** areas of the extreme west are the only parts of Ireland where Irish is spoken as the main everyday language, expecially in Connemara, the Aran Islands, parts of Achill Island, and the Mullet Peninsula. *Udaras na Gaeltachta* is the government investment and development body charged with the economic, social and cultural promotion of the Gaeltacht communities of Galway and Mayo, aiming to harness indigenous resources and modern technology to preserve a fragile **ethnic culture**.

COUNTY GALWAY

County Galway is divided by the **Corrib River**, with the wild mountainous country of the Connemara district lying to the west of the river and fertile farming lowlands to the east. The **Slieve Aughty Mountains** form the county's southern borderland.

DON'T MISS

*** Inis Mor: largest and most accessible of the beautiful, barren Aran Islands.
** Dunguaire Castle: miniature fortress by the sea which early this century became the home of poet Oliver St John Gogarty.
** Battle of Aughrim Interpretative Centre: the centre recounts the story of the final battle of the War of the Two Kings.
** Westport House: County Mayo's only stately home.

Opposite: *Galway City straddles the Corrib River, popular with anglers.*

Galway City **

The only large city in the west of Ireland, Galway straddles the Corrib River. The site has been settled since the 10th century and received its royal charter from **Richard III** of England in 1484. Today, although Galway is a busy, modern commercial and university city, its streets still retain much of their medieval character.

Built in 1320, the **Collegiate Church of St Nicholas** was extended in the 16th century, sacked by Cromwell's troops in 1652 and later restored. It is the largest medieval parish church still in use in Ireland, with tombstones from as early as the 12th century. Open April–September, Mon–Sat 09:00–17:45, Sun 13:00–17:45; October–March, Mon–Sat 10:00–16:00, Sun 13:00–16:00.

Rathbaun Farm *

Situated 30km (19 miles) south of Galway off the N18 at Ardrahan, this picturesque **thatched farmhouse** and **working sheep farm** is open to visitors year-round, daily on request. For information, *see* Useful Contacts, page 93.

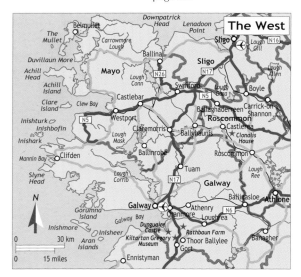

Thoor Ballylee **

Irish poet and playwright **W B Yeats** bought this Norman tower and cottage at Gort in 1916 and then made it his home in 1922. It became the subject of several of his poems. It has been carefully restored, and there is a multilingual audiovisual presentation, tearoom and bookshop. It is open from June–September, Monday–Saturday 09:30–17:00.

Kiltartan Gregory Museum ★

At Kiltartan Cross on the main N18 Galway-Limerick highway 3km north of Gort, this museum is located in a former schoolhouse. It contains first editions, manuscripts and photographs associated with the **Irish literary revival**. Open from 1 June to 30 September, daily 11:00–17:00.

Dunguaire Castle ★★

Built by the O'Hynes clan in 1520, this miniature fortress by the sea became the home early this century of poet **Oliver St John Gogarty**. Open from May–September, daily 09:30–17:30; medieval banquet twice nightly at 17:30 and 20:45.

Above: *W B Yeats made this Norman tower at Thoor Ballylee his home.*

Battle of Aughrim Interpretative Centre ★★

Off the N6 at Aughrim, near the battlefield, the centre recounts the story of the final battle of the **War of the Two Kings**, fought between the forces of William of Orange (William III of England) and James VII and II. Open April–September, Tuesday–Saturday 10:00–18:00, Sunday 14:00–18:00.

Aran Islands

Largest and most accessible of the beautiful, barren Aran Islands, **Inishmore** is crowned by the ancient stone fortresses of Dún Aengus and Dún Dúcathair, as well as a number of stone beehive huts used by the earliest Christian hermits. **Kilronan**, or Cill Rónáin, the main port, is reached by boat from Rossaveal (40 minutes) or Galway (90 minutes), or alternatively by air from Connemara Airport (6 minutes). The **Aran Heritage Centre** at Kilronan reveals the traditions of the Aran Islanders, which remained almost unchanged until the 20th century. Open April–May and September–October, daily 11:00–17:00; June–August, daily 10:00–19:00.

IRELAND IN FILM

Ireland has inspired many films, from the 1952 classic *The Quiet Man*, starring **John Wayne**, to films of the 1990s. In the last ten years alone, **Daniel Day Lewis** has starred in **Christy Brown's** autobiographical film *My Left Foot* (1989), and also in *In the Name of the Father* (1993). All three of **Roddy Doyle's** Barrytown books, *The Commitments* (1990), *The Snapper* (1992) and *The Van* (1995), have been filmed in Dublin, as has *Michael Collins* (1996), starring **Liam Neeson** in the title role. Ireland also stands in for other locations – the Wicklow Mountains were used for **Mel Gibson's** *Braveheart*, set in Scotland, and the beaches of Wexford substituted for those of Normandy in **Steven Spielberg's** *Saving Private Ryan* (1998).

Above: *Looking across Westport Bay towards Croagh Patrick.*

COUNTY MAYO

Mayo's dramatic coastline, tranquil lakes and open countryside make it one of the most appealing, and most untouched, counties in the Republic. Like so many Irish regions, Mayo offers something for everyone, from boating and angling to riding and walking. The county also contains two of Ireland's holiest shrines, at **Croagh Patrick** and at **Knock**. The coastal town of **Westport** is one of Ireland's most attractive historic towns.

MIRACULOUS APPARITION

In 1879, villagers from **Knock** in County Mayo reported that they had seen the **Virgin Mary** appear to them above the local church. Since then, Knock has become a major pilgrimage centre, with hundreds of thousands of visitors annually, among them **Pope John Paul II**, who came in 1979. Amazingly, this little village has its own international airport, the result of a campaign by the parish priest, **Father James Horan**, who persuaded the government to come up with 10 million euros to build it. Not only open to pilgrims, it makes a useful gateway to this part of Ireland, with charter flights from several British airports and further afield.

Westport ★★

Earmarked as one of Ireland's **heritage towns**, Westport strikes a remarkable contrast with its rural surroundings. Overlooking **Clew Bay** and the Atlantic and in turn overlooked by the crag of Croagh Patrick, the town's heart is the **Mall**, lined with gracious Georgian buildings. Westport is an unusual example of a planned Georgian town, with a street plan and many buildings laid out by the noted architect **James Wyatt** in the second quarter of the 18th century, under the patronage of the **Browne family**, later Earls of Altamont.

Set in several hectares of landscaped grounds, the dignified manor **Westport House**, seat of the Browne family, is County Mayo's only stately home. Designed by **Richard Cassells**, the original house dates from 1730. A fine collection of Georgian silver and furniture is on display inside. Open Monday–Sunday 11:30–17:00.

Croagh Patrick ★★

The mountain overlooks Westport and the bay and is one of Ireland's **holiest sites**, attracting thousands of devout pilgrims on the last Sunday in July, when they follow in the footsteps of **St Patrick** to the chapel at its peak, where the saint is said to have fasted for 40 days and nights.

Achill Island ★★★

Ireland's largest island, Achill Island is separated by a narrow strait from the Corraun Peninsula (crossed by road bridge) and has spectacular cliff walks, as well as sandy beaches at **Keem Bay** on its south coast and **Dugort** on its north coast.

Clare Island ★★★

Lying at the mouth of Clew Bay, Clare Island offers stunning **cliffscapes**, excellent **sea angling** and **scuba diving** in clear Atlantic waters. It is a wonderful place to soak up the atmosphere of this remote coastline, and attracts fewer crowds than well-known Achill.

National Marian Shrine, Knock ★★

Since the appearance of the Virgin Mary to a group of villagers in 1879, Knock has become a major **pilgrimage centre** attracting 1.5 million visitors annually, and as a result of the efforts of a local priest even has its own international airport to handle the pilgrim traffic. Among those who have visited the site is **Pope John Paul II**, who made it the climax of his 1979 visit to Ireland.

COUNTY ROSCOMMON

Roscommon today is a prosperous, inland **farming county** with little hint of its tragic past: it was among the counties worst affected by the **potato famine** of 1845, when many of its people perished and still more emigrated. Low-lying, its farmlands are interspersed with lakes, boglands and low hills. A quiet agricultural market centre, **Roscommon Town** was founded in the 6th century by Felim O'Conor, King of Connaught, and the missionary St Coman.

LAKE MONSTER

Like Scotland's Loch Ness, at least one Irish lough is said to have its own monster. In 1969, three local men (two of whom are still alive) at **Scaheens Lough** on **Achill Island** saw a 3m (10ft) long animal, standing 1m (3ft) high and with short brown hair, a long tail and sharp teeth. They described it as 'a mixture between a greyhound and a sheep'.

Below: *Sheep graze on the sparse pasture of remote Achill Island.*

CARAVAN HOLIDAYS

One of the best ways to see Ireland is on a slow-paced horse-drawn caravan holiday along the **rural back roads**. You drive a horse pulling a covered wagon that sleeps up to four, and you can also rent extra horses for accompanying riders. With its quiet roads and beautiful scenery, Ireland is particularly suited to this type of holiday. **Companies** specializing in such holidays include Clissman Horse Caravans, Carrigmore, Wicklow, tel: (0404) 48188, fax: (0404) 48288; Into the West, Pallas, Tynagh, Loughrea, County Galway, tel: (0509) 45147; Kilvahan Horse-drawn Caravans, Kilvahan, Portlaoise, County Laois, tel: (0502) 27048, fax: (0502) 27225; Mayo Horse-drawn Caravan Holidays, Belcarra, Castlebar, County Mayo, tel: (094) 32054, fax: (094) 32351; Slattery's Horse-drawn Caravans, 1 Russell Street, Tralee, County Kerry, tel: (066) 24088, fax: (066) 25981.

Below: *Exploring Ireland in a horse-drawn caravan.*

Clonalis House ★★

Just west of Castlerea, about 32km (20 miles) from Roscommon Town, the manor stands on the site of the castle of the O'Conor kings of Connaught, claimed to date from the reign of **Ferdach the Just** in the late 1st century AD. Built in the late 19th century, it is a hotch-potch of architectural styles – predominantly Victorian, Queen Anne and Italianate – and houses a collection of 10,000 important **historic documents**, from prayer books to poetry. Open June–September, daily 11:00–17:30.

King House Interpretative Centre ★★

King House, at Boyle, 50km (31 miles) north of Roscommon Town, was the 18th-century home of the Earls of Kingston. Abandoned at the end of the 18th century, it became an army barracks and now houses an interpretative centre concentrating on the history of the **Connaught region**, its chiefs and kings. It also deals with the history of the **King family**, owners of the house from 1603–1790, and of the **O'Conor dynasty** which, as well as ruling Connaught, included 11 of Ireland's High Kings. Open April–September, daily 10:00–18:00.

Strokestown Park House and Famine Museum ★★★

A magnificent neo-Palladian mansion built in the 1730s by **Richard Cassells**, who designed Leinster House in Dublin and many of the other great houses throughout Ireland, Strokestown Park was originally the estate of the Pakenham-Mahon family, local landowners, and has been painstakingly restored to its 18th-century grandeur. Next to it is the **Irish Famine Museum** which gives grim if fascinating insight into the disastrous failure of the potato crop and its far-reaching and tragic effects on Roscommon and the whole of Ireland. Open mid-March to mid-October, daily 10:30–17:30.

The West at a Glance

BEST TIMES TO VISIT

Best months are **May–Sep**. Jul–Aug are the busiest tourist months. Many attractions and guesthouses close in winter.

GETTING THERE

By Air: Direct flights from Dublin, London (Luton) and Manchester to Galway by Eastern Airways, and from London (Stansted), Manchester and Birmingham to Knock. Summer charter flights to Knock from Frankfurt, Düsseldorf, Munich and Zürich, May–Sep only.
By Road: The N4/N5 highway connects Roscommon and Mayo with Dublin. The N17 connects Galway to Knock in Mayo and points north, and the N6 connects Galway City to central Ireland and Dublin. Express buses connect towns.
By Rail: Rail services connect Westport, Castlebar, Boyle, Roscommon and Galway with central Ireland and Dublin.

GETTING AROUND

Bus services connect all main towns and villages in Galway, Mayo, Roscommon and neighbouring counties. Bus Eireann, Eyre Square Railway Station, Galway City, tel: (091) 562-000, fax: (091) 565-077.
Ferries to Aran Islands from Galway Docks daily in summer. Aran Ferries, 12 Eyre Square, Galway City, tel: (091) 568-903, fax: (091) 568-538. InisMór Ferries: www.aran direct.com

WHERE TO STAY

LUXURY
Cashel House Hotel, Galway Clifden Road, 2km (1 mile) west of Recess, Cashel, County Galway, tel: (095) 31001, fax: (095) 31077, e-mail: cashelhh@iol.ie Set in 16ha (40 acres) of grounds, private beach, tennis, fishing.
Enniscoe House, Castlehill, near Crossmolina, Ballina, County Mayo, tel: (096) 31112, fax: (096) 31773. Closed 14 October to 1 April. Family-owned heritage house on Lough Conn.

MID-RANGE
Currarevagh House, Oughterard, Connemara, County Galway, tel: (091) 552-312, fax: (091) 552-731. Victorian country manor on shores of Lough Corrib, with tennis, golf and angling. Closed 1 October to 1 April.

BUDGET
Acorn House, 19 Dublin Road, Galway, County Galway, tel/fax: (091) 770-990. Three-star city-centre guesthouse, affordable.
Angler's Rest, Castlebar Street, Westport, County Mayo, tel: (098) 25461, no fax. Amiable guesthouse in convenient location.

WHERE TO EAT

LUXURY
De Burgos Restaurant, 15–17 Augustine Street, Galway City, tel: (091) 562-188, no fax. Game, trout, salmon, European cuisine.
Ardmore House, The Quay, Westport, County Mayo, tel: (098) 25994, fax: (098) 25462. Fresh lobster, oysters, mussels and game in season.

MID-RANGE
Hooker Jimmy's, The Fishmarket, Spanish Arch, Galway City, tel: (091) 568-351, fax: (091) 568-352. Family-run riverside seafood restaurant.
Asgard Tavern and Restaurant, The Quay, Westport, County Mayo, tel: (098) 25319, no fax. Award-winning pub-style fisherman's restaurant.

BUDGET
Lavelles, Bridge Street, County Mayo, tel: (098) 26049. Family-run pub on Westport's main shopping street.

USEFUL CONTACTS

Ireland West Tourism, Forster Street, Galway, tel: (091) 537-700, fax: (091) 537-733. For hotel bookings, e-mail: booking@western-tourism.ie For information on **Rathbaun Farm**, Ardrahan, tel: (091) 635-385.
Mayo Tourist Information, Westport, tel: (098) 25711, fax: (098) 26709.
Roscommon Tourist Information, Boyle, tel: (079) 62145, no fax.
Information Department, Shrine Office, Knock, County Mayo, tel: (094) 88100, fax: (094) 88295.

7
The Midlands

Golf, fishing and pony trekking are some attractions of Longford, Westmeath, Offaly and Laois (pronounced 'leash'), the four landlocked counties clustered in the heart of Ireland. The **Royal Canal** passes through County Westmeath on its way to join the **Shannon** on the borders of the region, and the northern branch of the **Grand Canal** passes through County Offaly and its county town, **Tullamore**. Longford and Westmeath are lakeland counties, with the wide **Lough Ree**, one of the chain of lakes formed by the Shannon Waterway.

COUNTIES LAOIS AND OFFALY
Portlaoise

The county town, whose name means 'Fort of Laois', was fought over many times in the centuries following the Norman invasion of Ireland. Occupying a strategic location in the centre of the county (and of Ireland), it was fortified during the reign of **Mary Tudor** ('Bloody Mary' to the English but remembered more kindly in Catholic Ireland). Just outside the town centre is the **Rock of Dunamase**, crowned by the ruins of a **medieval castle** destroyed during the Cromwellian invasion of 1650.

Abbeyleix

Abbeyleix is a designated **heritage town**, graced by fine 19th-century architecture, including a fine **church** built in 1895 in imitation of Pugin's church at Arles, and **Abbeyleix House and Gardens** (not open to the public), home of the aristocratic de Vesci family.

DON'T MISS

** **Carrigglass Manor:** splendid 19th-century mock-Tudor castle.
** **Emo Court Demesne:** fine 18th-century mansion with magnificent interior, standing in landscaped gardens.
*** **Birr Castle Demesne and Historic Science Centre:** one of Ireland's most spectacular gardens, with a historic observatory, now Ireland's first Historic Science Centre.
** **Athlone Castle Visitor Centre:** 13th-century castle, military museum and interpretative centre.

Opposite: *The Shannon-Erne, one of Europe's longest waterways.*

Above: *Birr Gardens is home to more than 1000 different trees and shrubs.*

Portarlington

Standing on the **River Barrow**, Portarlington has one foot in County Offaly and the other in County Laois. It was founded in the 17th century by English settlers. **French Huguenot Protestants**, fleeing religious persecution in France, were settled here in the late 17th century and their descendants still spoke French until the mid-19th century. A **French festival** in July each year celebrates this French connection.

Emo Court Demesne **

Designed in the Palladian style in 1790 by **James Gandon**, the architect of many of Dublin's finest buildings, Emo Court and its demesne (estate) was to be the home of the Earl of Portarlington, who was killed in the abortive rebellion of 1798. The interior is adorned with marble and giltwork, with a fine domed reception room. Open June–September 10:30–18:00; gardens open year-round, daily 10:30–17:30.

Birr Castle Demesne and Historic Science Centre ***

The spectacular grounds of Birr Castle have more than 1000 different kinds of tree and shrub, and the world's tallest box hedges. The **castle observatory**, built in 1845, houses a giant 183cm (72in) reflecting telescope, once the largest in the world. Restored in 1997, it is now part of Ireland's first **Historic Science Centre**. Open daily 09:00–18:00 (year-round).

Cloghan Castle, Banagher **

At the junction of the Shannon and Little Brosna rivers, the original **medieval castle** was a stronghold of the O'Madden clan. It has been added to since then, and is still a private home, standing in a **landscaped park**, with its fine historic furniture, paintings and antiques. Open May–September, Wednesday–Sunday 14:00–18:00.

OLIVER GOLDSMITH

Born in County Longford, Oliver Goldsmith (1730–74) was the rebellious son of an Irish clergyman. He ran away from **Trinity College** (selling his books to pay his way) and drifted around Europe before being taken up by the London literary clique of **Dr Samuel Johnson**. A prolific writer, he published hundreds of plays, essays and histories. Best known among them are *The Vicar of Wakefield* (1766) and *She Stoops to Conquer* (1773), which are still performed.

Clonmacnoise Monastery, Shannonbridge ★★

In AD548–9, the missionary **St Ciaran** founded one of Ireland's great monasteries here beside the River Shannon. Many of the most famous **illuminated manuscripts**, including the 11th-century *Annals of Tigernach* and the 12th-century *Book of the Dun Cow*, were written by monks of Clonmacnoise. Around the ruined cathedral stand smaller chapels, a round tower, Celtic crosses and early Christian grave slabs. An **Interpretative Centre** with audiovisual show fills you in on the historic background. Open daily 09:00–17:30.

Clonmacnoise and West Offaly Railway ★★

There is a 9km (5.5-mile) **guided rail tour**, with commentary, through one of the most important surviving stretches of Irish **raised bogland**, with unique flora and fauna including oak trees of 6000 years old. Open from 1 April to 31 October, with tours running daily from Clonmacnoise, every hour on the hour, 10:00–17:00.

COUNTY WESTMEATH
Mullingar

A sprightly **market town**, Mullingar is close to the lakes of Westmeath, with Lough Ennell to the south and Lough Owell, Lough Iron and Lough Derravaragh just to the north, a location that makes it a popular base for anglers. It stands on the **Royal Canal**, which passes just south of the town centre. The **Market House Museum** is a local history museum with farming and fishing equipment, household accoutrements, tools, photographs and paintings. Open June–September, Monday–Friday 10:00–17:30, Saturday 10:00–12:30.

Locke's Distillery Museum ★

At Kilbeggan, 25km (15.5 miles) east of Athlone, is one of the world's oldest licensed whiskey distilleries. Closed in the early 1950s, it has been reopened as a museum, with guided tours of the **antiquated coppers** and **stills** used for almost 200 years. Open daily May–October 09:00–18:00, November–March 10:00–16:00.

GONE FISHING

Ireland offers some of Europe's finest fishing, whether for the noble **salmon** or the humble **perch**. Coarse fishermen will find bream, rudd, roach, tench, dace, perch, eel and carp in **lakes** and **rivers**, with a year-round open season and no licence required in most parts of the country. The hgue **pike** that haunt Irish waters are the stuff of legend, and pike over 9kg (20 lb) are often taken, with 14kg (30 lb) fish caught regularly. There is **game angling** too, for salmon, brown trout and sea trout. A **state licence** is required for salmon and sea trout and costs from 3.80 euros per day (or 12.70 euros for three weeks). Most salmon and trout fisheries are privately owned and permits cost from around 38 euros. Sea anglers will find everything from cod and conger to skate and blue shark.

MULLINGAR REBELS

Feelings can still run high when relics of the 1916 **Easter Rising** are not given due respect. When Mullingar's 19th-century **Market House**, in the town centre, was renovated in 1999, the town council removed the **plaque** above the main door commemorating local men who had taken part in the Rising. The council caused local outrage with a plan to remount the plaque inside the building, and after protests, petitions and letters to the press, it was restored to pride of place, where it can be seen today.

Below: *The monastery at Clonmacnoise, founded in the 6th century.*

Athlone Castle Visitor Centre ★★

Built in 1210 for the English King John, the castle contains a **military museum** and **interpretative centre** with an audiovisual display about the life of the great Irish tenor, **John McCormack** (1884–1945), some of whose possessions – including his gramophone – are on show in the **Castle Folk Museum**. Open April–September, daily 10:00–16:30.

Belvedere House, Tyrrellspass ★

Designed in the mid-18th century by the leading Irish architect of the Palladian style, **Richard Cassels**, for Robert Rochfort, Earl of Belvedere, the house has fine stuccowork within, belying its modest size. It stands in its own **gardens**, which are maintained in the style of the period, with grottoes and rockeries. Open March–April and September–October, daily 10:00–18:00, May–August 09:30–21:00, November–February, daily 10:30–16:30.

COUNTIES LONGFORD AND MONAGHAN
Longford

On the banks of the **River Camlin**, the county town of Longford has little of note, but 5km (3 miles) from the town is the attractive **Carrigglas Manor**. Built between 1790 and 1830, in mock-Tudor Gothic style, Carrigglas was and still is the home of the Lefroy family. Its magnificent interior now houses a fine collection of family portraits, Victorian costumes and lace. Open June–September, Thursday–Monday 14:00–18:30.

Monaghan

A tidy farming town, Monaghan's sturdy 18th- and 19th-century buildings date from a period of some prosperity from farming, weaving and lacemaking. At the **Monaghan County Museum** the big attraction is the bronze **Cross of Clogher**, a superb 13th-century altar relic. Other displays highlight the town's past prosperity, and the lace and linen-weaving crafts. Open Monday–Friday 11:00–17:00, Saturday 12:00–17:00.

The Midlands at a Glance

By Road: Bus Eireann operates frequent bus services from Dublin to all major towns in the region and connects the main towns within the region.
By Rail: Irish Rail trains connect Portlaoise, Mullingar, Longford and Athlone with Dublin and points south, east and west of the region.

LUXURY
Kinnitty Castle Demesne,
Kinnitty, Birr, County Offaly, tel: (579) 137318, fax: (579) 137284. Castle hotel on estate offering riding, tennis, walking and clay shooting.
The Heritage-Portlaoise,
tel: (578) 678588, fax: (578) 678577. One of the most luxurious hotels in the area, and a popular conference venue, it features a spa, leisure centre and two restaurants.
Bridge House Hotel and Leisure Club, Tullamore, County Offaly, tel: (579) 322000, fax: (579) 325690. Hotel complex with gym, swimming pool and sauna.

MID-RANGE
Longford Arms Hotel, Main Street, Longford, tel: (043) 46296, fax: (043) 46244. Comfortable modern hotel with award-winning café.
O'Loughlin's Hotel, 30 Main St, Portlaoise, County Laois, tel: (0502) 21305, fax: (0502) 60883. Comfortable, family-run small hotel and pub.

BUDGET
Castle Arms Hotel,
The Square, Durrow, County Laois, tel: (578) 736117. Family-run hotel with golf and fishing nearby.
Maltings Guesthouse,
Castle Street, Birr, County Offaly, tel: (579) 121345, fax: (579) 122073. Very attractive guesthouse by the river and castle.
Sea Dew Guesthouse,
Clonminch Road, Tullamore, County Offaly, tel/fax: (579) 352054. Modern purpose-built guesthouse, only about five minutes' walk from the town centre.

LUXURY
Le Chateau, The Docks, Athlone, County Westmeath, tel: (0902) 94517. Riverside restaurant in old church, steak and fish.

MID-RANGE
The Bridge House, Bridge Street, Tullamore, County Offaly, tel: (579) 322000. Carvery restaurant and coffee shop.
Bellamy's Restaurant, Main Street, Portlaoise, County Laois, tel: (578) 622303. Old-world bar, with good home-cooked food.
Conlon's Restaurant, 5–9 Dublingate Street, Athlone, County Westmeath, tel: (0902) 74376. Specializes in traditional Irish dishes at reasonable prices.

Treacy's, The Heath,
Portlaoise, County Laoise, tel: (0502) 46535, fax: (0502) 46781. The oldest pub in Ireland to be run continuously under the same family name, Treacy's is renowned for its slap-up Sunday lunches.
Dr Cuppaiges, The Tanyard, Moate, County Westmeath. Newly refurbished pub and restaurant, Irish and international dishes, live traditional music four nights a week, tel: (0902) 81790, no fax.

BUDGET
The Left Bank Bistro, Bastion Street, Athlone, County Westmeath, tel: (0902) 94446. Recommended café-restaurant with good wine list.
The Gramby, 9 Dominick Street, Mullingar, County Westmeath, tel: (044) 40280. Good value pub-restaurant.

Midlands-East Tourism Information Offices linked into the **Gulliver** information and reservations computer service are at the following:
Longford
Longford Tourist Office, Main Street, Longford, tel: (043) 46566.
Mullingar
Mullingar Tourist Office,
Dublin Road, Mullingar, tel: (044) 48650, fax: (044) 40413.
Portlaoise
Portlaoise Tourist Office,
James Fintan Lawlor Avenue, Portlaoise, tel: (0502) 21178.

8
The Northwest

The counties of Ireland's northwest include Leitrim, with its lakes, rivers and canals; Sligo, with beaches and landscapes that inspired Ireland's greatest 19th-century poet; and wild Donegal, with its staggering grandeur.

COUNTY SLIGO

Sligo has plenty of variety, from the slopes of the **Daltry Mountains**, rising to 650m (2133ft), to the sandy **Atlantic beaches** of Sligo Bay, some of which – like Strandhill, Easky and Enniscrone – are reckoned among Europe's finest surfing and boardsailing spots. Its scenery inspired the poet **W B Yeats**, who asked to be buried beneath the summit of Benbulben, which looks out over the Atlantic.

Sligo Town

Straddling the **River Garavogue**, Sligo has an attractive 18th-century town centre. The biggest town in the region, it has plenty to see. **Sligo Abbey** contains the ruins of a Dominican priory founded in the mid-13th century, destroyed by fire, rebuilt in the 15th century, and sacked by Cromwell's soldiery in 1641. Inside the walls are graceful **cloisters**, as well as 15th- and 16th-century **tombs**. Open March–October, daily 10:00–18:00, November–February, Friday–Sunday 09:30–16:30 .

In **Sligo County Museum and Municipal Art Gallery**, the **Yeats Room** celebrates the life of the poet, with a huge and eclectic collection of his writings, newspaper cuttings, letters and photographs. Upstairs, the art gallery houses paintings by the poet's brother, Jack B Yeats. Open

Opposite: *Dry stone walls divide almost equally stony fields high in the Derryveagh Mountains.*

Right: *W B Yeats is buried in the shadow of Benbulben, in the churchyard at Drumcliff.*

W B YEATS

The **poet** William Butler Yeats (1865–1939) was prominent in the campaign to revive a distinctive Irish culture, establishing the **Abbey Theatre** as a national institution and, after the 1916 Rising, eulogizing its martyrs in his verse. He was awarded the **Nobel Prize** for Literature in 1923 and became a Free State **senator** (1922–28). In 1932 he founded the **Irish Academy of Letters**.

JACK B YEATS

Ireland's finest **painter**, Jack B Yeats, was born in London and brought up in **County Sligo**, the landscapes, light and colours of which had as deep an effect on his painting as on the poetry of his brother, W B Yeats. **Horses** were a favourite subject in his later oil paintings, symbolizing loyalty, freedom, intelligence and strength. His **style** is characterized by thick, powerful brush strokes and vibrant light and shade.

June–September, Tuesday–Saturday 10:00–12:00, 14:00–16:50; October–May, Tuesday–Saturday 14:00–16:50.

Lough Gill

The River Garavogue flows out of Lough Gill into the Atlantic only 3km (2 miles) away. The lake, attractive in its own right, has in it, less than 100m (109yd) off the south shore, a tiny island – **Innisfree** – which inspired one of W B Yeats's best known poems, *The Lake Isle of Innisfree*. Boat trips on the lake depart from Parke's Castle.

Some 10km (6 miles) east of Sligo Town, on the shores of Lough Gill, **Parke's Castle** is a fortified house of the Plantation era, when English Protestant landlords built homes they could defend against their Irish tenants, who often rose against them. It has been well restored, and has a lovely setting. Open daily March–October 10:00–18:00.

Dating from around 3000BC, the **Deer Park Court Cairn** tomb stands close to the shore of the lake, midway between Parke's Castle and Sligo Town. It contains three **burial chambers**, but these are not open to visitors.

Strandhill

About 8km (5 miles) from Sligo Town, Strandhill is at the tip of a peninsula stretching out into Sligo Bay. Atlantic combers pound its sandy beaches, making it more attractive to **surfers** than to swimmers. Just offshore – you can walk to it at low tide – is the original **Coney Island**, which locals claim gave its name to the

New York suburb famed for its amusement park.

Just 1km (0.5 mile) east of Strandhill is the enormous Stone-Age graveyard of **Carrowmore**, with more than 60 Mesolithic and Neolithic stone circles and passage graves. Open May–October, daily 10:00–18:00.

Maeve's Cairn is a hilltop monument on **Knocknarea Mountain**, 2km (1 mile) northwest of the Carrowmore site. Local legend says it is the tomb of the legendary **Celtic Queen Maeve**, built around the time of Christ. Archaeologists believe it may conceal a huge passage grave similar to that at **Newgrange**, County Meath (*see* page 60). The site is not enclosed, but has never been excavated so can only be seen from the outside.

County Leitrim

Lough Allen, northernmost of the lakes of the Shannon Waterway, divides County Leitrim in two. On its east side, the **Iron Mountains** divide the county from its low-lying southern neighbour, County Longford. To the north is County Fermanagh in Northern Ireland, with a narrow corridor connecting County Leitrim with County Donegal, the northernmost county in the Republic.

Carrick-on-Shannon

Carrick's location could hardly be bettered and in summer it is a busy base for people cruising the **Shannon-Erne Waterway**. Starting at **Leitrim**, about 4km (2.5 miles) north of here, the waterway connects a chain of loughs all the way to **Upper Lough Erne**, on the border with Northern Ireland, and passes under 34 stone

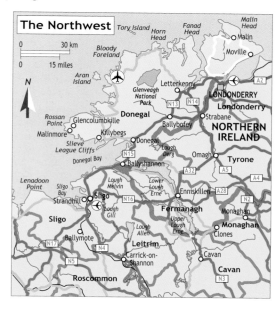

The Northwest

bridges and through 16 locks on the recently reopened **Ballinamore-Ballyconnell Canal**, restored in the 1990s after 120 years of neglect.

Leitrim Heritage Centre and Museum, Ballinamore ★

Housed in the county library on Ballinamore's main street, the centre's main activity is helping the descendants of Leitrim emigrants to trace their local **ancestry**. The small museum in the same building immortalizes Leitrim's role in the 1916 **Easter Rising**, when the county was one of the few areas outside Dublin to take up arms against the British.

COUNTY DONEGAL

Best known for its **tweed**, Donegal is one of Ireland's wildest, remotest counties, almost cut off from the rest of the Republic by the salient of Fermanagh and connected to County Sligo only by a narrow corridor. Donegal forms two anvil-shaped peninsulas with a coastline that runs roughly northeast, with **Donegal Bay** to the south, **Lough Foyle** to the north, and **Lough Swilly** dividing the larger part of the county from the **Inishowen Peninsula**. At the tip of Inishowen, **Malin Head** – a familiar name to anyone who listens to the shipping forecasts – is the northernmost point of the island of Ireland.

Donegal is Ireland's second-largest county, but is quite sparsely populated, and its attractions are more scenic than man-made, including its fine **beaches** and towering **sea cliffs**.

Donegal

Like many towns on the coasts of Ireland, Donegal was originally a **Viking** settlement. Its Irish name, 'Dún na nGall', means 'Fortress of the Foreigners'. With a handful of sights of its own, Donegal is also a good base for fishing, golf, touring and pony trekking.

Donegal Castle was originally built in 1474 by Red Hugh O'Donnell, Prince of Tyrconnell. The ruined castle is on a rock overlooking the **River Eske**. It also includes a **fortified tower** dating from 1505 and a **Jacobean house** built in 1610 by Sir Basil Brooke, the English squire who was granted the castle after the defeat of Red Hugh's descendant, Hugh Roe O'Donnell, in the Elizabethan conquest of Ireland in the late 16th century. Open March–October, daily 10:00–18:00.

Slieve League Cliffs

About 35km (22 miles) west of Donegal Town, the awesome Slieve League cliffs, dropping vertically some 300m (984ft) into the Atlantic below a 606m (1988ft) summit, are **Europe's highest sea cliffs**. The best viewing point out to sea is at **Bunglass**, signposted from the R263 coast road.

Glencolumbkille Folk Village and Heritage Centre ★

Just outside the village of Glencolumbkille, 40km (25 miles) from Donegal Town on the R263, the Heritage Centre commemorates the life of the missionary **St Colmcille** (St Columba), who is said to have lived here in the 6th century and who went on to found the Christian centre of Iona, in the Scottish Hebrides, and begin the Christianization of Scotland. A pilgrimage site in summer, it attracts devout Catholics.

Set up to help revive a dwindling community in the 1970s, the Folk Village has replicas of **thatched cottages** furnished as they would have been in the 19th century. Open April–September, Monday–Saturday 10:00–18:00, Sunday 12:00–18:00.

Lough Derg Visitor Centre ★

Lough Derg, 20km (12 miles) east of Donegal Town, has an importance to devout **Catholics** out of all proportion to its size. In **pilgrimage** season (June–August) tens of thousands of penitents repeat **St Patrick's** reputed period of

Above: *Donegal tweed is one of the finest woollen cloths you can buy.*
Opposite: *The folk village and heritage centre at Glencolumbkille.*

DONEGAL TWEED

Donegal tweed is a fine Irish product. Originally a heavy-duty woollen cloth for all weathers – its close weave and high **lanolin** content made it waterproof as well as warm – it was taken up by the Anglo-Irish gentry as suitable **country wear** for walking, shooting and fishing, and later acquired international cachet. To meet modern demand, it is now made in **lighter** weights too, in a wide range of natural shades, and can be bought throughout Ireland, either by length or made up into suits, jackets, skirts or caps.

Above: *The dramatic Atlantic coastline at Glencolumbkille in County Donegal.*

fasting on the tiny island in the lake. The Lough Derg Visitor Centre provides the background to the story. Open Apr–Sep, Mon–Sat 10:00–17:00, Sun 12:00–17:00.

Letterkenny

Letterkenny is the largest town in County Donegal (it, not Donegal, is the county town). Located at the head of **Lough Swilly**, a long, narrow fjord leading to the Atlantic, the town is a very convenient base for exploring the northern tip of Ireland. **Donegal County Museum**, located on the High Street, is a small museum containing local relics and finds, displays of weaving and tweed-making, and local photographs. Open Monday–Friday 10:00–16:30, Saturday 13:00–16:30.

Glenveagh National Park ★★

Some 16km (10 miles) west of Letterkenny on the R251, Glenveagh National Park comprises about 10,000ha (24,710 acres) of lakes, bogs and also the **Derrivale Mountains**, rising to the 752m (2467ft) peak of **Errigal**. In the 19th century the park was the estate of the unpopular landlord **George Adair**, who evicted his tenants in 1861 to turn it into a deer forest. He also imported rhododendrons, and built himself a mock-baronial manor, **Glenveagh Castle**, in imitation of Balmoral, Queen Victoria's residence on Deeside in Scotland. The castle, red deer and rhododendrons are still there, and the castle is surrounded by fine gardens. Glenveagh Castle and Visitor Centre open Mar–Oct, daily 10:00–18:30 (last admission 17:00).

Inishowen

The anvil-shaped Inishowen Peninsula, lying between Lough Foyle and Lough Swilly, ends at **Malin Head**, the northernmost point of Ireland. Wonderfully desolate, the headland really feels like the end of the world.

The Northwest at a Glance

By Air: Flights from London, Manchester and Dublin to Londonderry, just across the border from Letterkenny.
By Bus: Bus Eireann from Sligo to Donegal and Letterkenny. Cross-border bus services between Donegal and Strabane in Northern Ireland and between Donegal, Letterkenny and Derry in Northern Ireland. Bus Eireann from Dublin to Leinster and Sligo, and from Sligo to Castlebar and Galway.

By Bus: Bus Eireann services connect all major towns.

LUXURY
Markree Castle, Collooney, County Sligo, tel: (071) 916-7800. Wonderfully grand 19th-century castle with fine restaurant and gardens.
Coppershill House, Riverstown, County Sligo, tel: (071) 916-5108, fax: (071) 916-5466. Still run by the O'Hara family seven generations after it was built in 1774, this Georgian mansion stands in a 202ha (500-acre) estate. Boating, fishing, tennis, elegant bedrooms.
Sand House Hotel, Rossnowlagh, County Donegal, tel: (071) 985-1777, fax: (071) 985-2100. Small four-star on 3km (2-mile) beach with three championship golf courses nearby.

MID-RANGE
Rathmullan House, Rathmullan, County Donegal, tel: (074) 915-8188, fax: (074) 915-8200. Superb location beside Lough Swilly, indoor heated pool, friendly and informal country house.
Clarence Hotel, Wine Street, Sligo, tel: (071) 914-2211, fax: (071) 914-5823. Centrally located in striking historic listed building.

BUDGET
Aisleigh Guest House, Dublin Road, Carrick-on-Shannon, County Leitrim, tel: (078) 912-0313, fax: (078) 912-0313. Welcoming three-star guesthouse.
Bush Hotel, Carrick-on-Shannon, County Leitrim, tel: (078) 912-0014, fax: (078) 912-1180, cheap hotel in convenient location.

LUXURY
Markree Castle (*see* Where to Stay above). Magnificent gilded dining room, Irish and French cuisine.
Harvey's Point Country Hotel and Restaurant, Lough Eske, Donegal Town (signposted on N66), tel: (073) 912-2208. Both Irish and French menus available. Recommended.
Restaurant St John's, Fahan, Inishowen, County Donegal, tel: (077) 916-0289, one of the finest places to eat in this part of Ireland.

MID-RANGE
Smugglers Creek Inn, Rossnowlagh, County Donegal, tel: (072) 915-2366. Award-winning pub-restaurant.
Embassy Rooms, John F Kennedy Parade, Sligo, tel: (071) 916-1250. Wholesome food, comfortable surroundings, riverside location.

BUDGET
Belshade Restaurant, The Diamond, Donegal Town, tel: (073) 912-2660. Home cooking, good soup and seafood.

Cruising the Shannon Shannon-Erne Waterway Promotions, Golf Links Road, Ballinamore, County Leitrim, tel: (078) 914-4855, fax: (078) 914-4856.
Tara Cruisers, Carrick-on-Shannon, County Leitrim, tel: (078) 912-1369, fax: (078) 912-1284.
Riversdale Barge Holidays, Ballinamore, County Leitrim, tel: (078) 914-4122, fax: (078) 914-4813.

Letterkenny
Northwest Tourism Information Office, Blaney Road, Letterkenny, tel: (074) 912-1160, fax: (074) 912-5180.
Sligo
Northwest Tourism Information Office, Aras Reddan, Temple Street, Sligo, tel: (071) 916-1201, fax: (071) 916-0360.

9
Northern Ireland

Northern Ireland's scenery, and the friendliness of its people, outweigh the 'Troubles' of the last 30 years. The six counties of **Ulster** – Derry, Antrim, Down, Armagh, Fermanagh and Tyrone – cover an area of 14,249km² (5500 sq miles) in the northeast corner of Ireland, some 130km (81 miles) north to south and 165km (103 miles) east to west. In the centre is the largest lake in Ireland, **Lough Neagh**. To the east, the **Irish Sea** narrows to a channel 20km (12 miles) wide between Torr Head in County Down and the Mull of Kintyre in Scotland. To the south, the fabled **Mountains of Mourne**, peaking at a little under 914m (3000ft), lend drama to the landscape, as do the harsh cliffs of the Antrim coast. Fascinating sights include Neolithic tombs, monkish round towers, Norman and Elizabethan castles and early Christian crosses. Most of the people live in the two main cities, **Belfast** and **Londonderry**, and in a handful of smaller towns, so there is plenty of unspoilt countryside.

BELFAST

During the 19th century, Belfast became an industrial city, known for its engineering and shipbuilding. Triumphalist murals of IRA gunmen or the Unionist hero King Billy (William of Orange) mark Nationalist and Loyalist neighbourhoods, but Belfast, the Troubles aside, is notably crime-free. Belfast stands at the head of **Belfast Lough**, a long, deep natural harbour on the east coast, between Antrim, Northern Ireland's northernmost county, and east-facing County Down.

DON'T MISS

★★★ Carrickfergus Castle: the finest surviving Norman castle in Northern Ireland.
★★★ Giant's Causeway: this formation of weirdly geometric basalt columns, sculpted by cooling lava, is a World Heritage Site.
★★★ Dunluce Castle: a magnificently sited clifftop castle.
★★★ Derry Walls: a ring of 17th-century ramparts surrounding the city centre.

Opposite: *The dour ramparts of Carrickfergus Castle, the finest Norman stronghold in the North.*

Opposite: Belfast Castle is a 19th century pastiche of a medieval stronghold.

Belfast City Hall ★

This Classical Renaissance building on Donegall Square in the city centre dates from 1906. Its 35m (115ft) **dome** and façade are matched within by a lavish **marble interior**. Guided tours Monday–Friday 11:00, 14:00 and 15:00; Saturday 14:00 and 15:00 (year-round).

Linen Hall Library ★

Also on Donegall Square, the library was built in 1788 and houses Irish and local **history** and **literary collections**. It is an excellent place to read up on Northern Ireland's complex recent history. Open Monday–Friday 09:30–17:30.

Lagan Weir Lookout ★★

An interactive visitors' centre overlooking Lagan Weir, Belfast's 5km (3-mile) long city-centre **water feature**, stands on Donegall Quay, site of the first Belfast village. Open April–September, Monday–Friday 11:00–17:00, Saturday 12:00–17:00, Sunday 14:00–17:00; October–March, Monday–Friday 11:00–15:30, Saturday 13:00–16:30, Sunday 14:00–16:30.

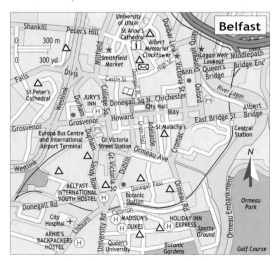

Ulster Museum ★★

Surrounded by the attractive **Botanic Gardens**, the museum has excellent **Irish art** and archeological collections which include a treasure trove from the **Spanish Armada** and an Early Ireland gallery. Closed for renovations until 2009.

The People's Museum (Fernhill House) ★★

This museum on Shankill Road has displays on the history of the staunchly Protestant and Unionist working-class heartland, the **Shankill district**, from the partition of Ireland through World War II. Open Monday–Saturday 10:00–16:00, Sunday 13:00–16:00.

Stormont Parliament Buildings ★★

The Stormont building, 5km (3 miles) from the city centre on Upper Newtownards Road, was the symbol of Ulster's Protestant ascendancy until the **Northern Ireland Parliament** was disbanded. Stormont is scheduled once again to become the seat of the new **Northern Ireland Assembly**, this time with power shared between Unionist and Nationalist representatives.

Belfast Castle ★★

This 19th-century mansion was built for the Earl of Donegall in the style of a medieval castle, with square keep and turrets. The castle has its own **heritage centre** and **antique shop**. On Antrim Road, the castle also has **panoramic views** of Belfast. Open Monday–Friday 09:00–22:00, Saturday 09:00–17:30.

COUNTY ANTRIM

Antrim's attractions include miles of cliffs and beaches, castles and modern visitor centres. The high point of a visit is the **Giant's Causeway**. Inland, the nine **Antrim Glens** are a startlingly beautiful pocket wilderness of rushing streams, woodland and waterfalls.

BUILT IN BELFAST

Built in the Belfast yard of **Harland and Wolff** for White Star Line and launched on 31 May 1911, the 45,000 tonne, 271m (890ft) *Titanic* was half as large again as her rivals, the Cunard liners *Lusitania* and *Mauritania*. Extra-large berths and gantries had to be built at the shipyard before construction of the ship could begin, and in New York the White Star piers had to be lengthened to accommodate her. She never arrived. On 10 April 1912, after her fitting-out in Belfast, she started her maiden voyage from Southampton. Her first, and last, port of call was **Cherbourg**, County Cork, on 11 April. Three days later, 640km (398 miles) off the coast of Newfoundland, *Titanic* struck an iceberg, rupturing six of her watertight compartments, and began to sink. With more than 2200 people on board, the ship had space aboard its lifeboats for only 1178 (200 more than the outdated British Board of Trade rule required), and 1517 lives were lost.

Above: *The Giant's Causeway's angular basalt pillars were formed by volcanic action.*

Carrickfergus ★★★

Carrickfergus, 20km (12 miles) northeast of Belfast, is still partially surrounded by its 17th-century ramparts. **Carrickfergus Castle**, with its 30m (98ft) tower, is the finest surviving Norman castle in Northern Ireland, built in 1180 by the Anglo-Norman baron **John de Courcy**. Open during April–September, Monday–Saturday 10:00–18:00, Sunday 14:00–18:00; October–March, Monday–Saturday 10:00–16:00, Sunday 14:00–16:00. At Heritage Plaza on Antrim Street, Carrickfergus, the **Knight Ride** monorail takes visitors back in time through the town's eight centuries of history. Open April–September, Monday–Saturday 10:00–18:00, Sunday 12:00–18:00; October–March, same days but closes 17:00.

Giant's Causeway ★★★

About 3km (2 miles) north of Bushmills Village, this basalt rock formation is a **World Heritage site**. The Causeway Visitors' Centre is open July–August 10:00–19:00, the rest of the year 10:00–sunset. The angular pillars of the Causeway were actually formed by volcanic action, but the ancient Irish had another explanation: they maintained the rocky 'road' was the work of the gigantic warrior **Finn MacCool**, who built it to link Ulster with the Scottish island of Staffa, home of a giantess whom Finn loved.

Old Bushmills Distillery ★★★

The **world's oldest whiskey distillery** has been in operation since 1608, making some of the finest and most distinctive whiskeys. Open April–October, Monday–Saturday 09:30–17:30, Sunday 12:00–17:00; tours are usually from November–March at 10:00, 11:00, 12:00, 13:30, 14:30, 15:30.

VOLCANIC ARGUMENT

Not until after heated debate during the 18th and 19th centuries did geologists finally agree that the angular pillars of the **Giant's Causeway** were formed by **volcanic action**. For the ancient Irish, however, the answer was much simpler: the rocky 'road' was the work of the gigantic, mythical warrior **Finn MacCool**, who built it to link **Ulster** with the Scottish island of **Staffa**, home of a female giant whom Finn loved.

Dunluce Castle ★★★

The largest castle in Northern Ireland stands on a cliff-top above the Atlantic, between Bushmills and nearby Portrush. Now a **picturesque ruin**, Dunluce was built between the 13th and 16th centuries by the **MacDonnells of Antrim**, who abandoned it in the late 17th century. Open April–September, daily 10:00–17:30; October–March, daily 10:00–16:30.

COUNTIES DERRY AND TYRONE

Home to Ulster's second city, County Derry also has wide expanses of open country, especially in the barren **Sperrin Mountains** in the very centre of the county, where the highest peak in the range, **Sawel**, reaches a height of 683m (2240ft).

The furthest west and the least populous of the six counties of Northern Ireland, Tyrone is a region of **empty moors** and scattered farms. The county is rich in **relics**, with more than 1000 Neolithic standing stones, stone circles and tall Irish crosses, erected between the 7th and 12th centuries.

Derry (Londonderry)

Standing on **Lough Foyle**, near the border with the Republic, Derry was founded by **St Columba** in AD546 and then became an English stronghold in the early 17th century, receiving the royal charter which added 'London' to its name in 1613. Behind its walls, up to 8m (26ft) high and 10m (33ft) wide, Londonderry withstood repeated sieges, in 1641, 1648 and 1689, when Derry declared for William of Orange. The **ramparts**, with their four original gates and muzzle-loading cannon, are intact.

SEAMUS HEANEY

Born in **Derry** in 1939, Seamus Heaney is not only Ireland's **greatest living poet** but perhaps the greatest now working in the English language. His first work, *Death of a Naturalist*, published in 1966, was influenced by Dublin poet **Patrick Kavanagh** and Englishman **Ted Hughes**. Accessibility is one of the keynotes of Heaney's work, which often deals with rural or natural themes. In 1995 he received the **Nobel Prize for Literature** and was also mooted as a possible British Poet Laureate, an honour which he made clear he would not accept.

Below: *Dunluce is the largest castle in Northern Ireland, with a dramatic clifftop setting.*

BRIAN FRIEL

Brian Friel is Ireland's best-known living **playwright**. He has written more than 20 plays since 1964, when his first, *Philadelphia, Here I Come!*, was performed in Dublin. In 1989 he set up the **Field Day Theatre Company** with Seamus Heaney, Stephen Rea and others, and in 1998 his *Dancing at Lughnasa* (1990), was made into a film starring Meryl Streep.

The main attraction and showpiece of the **Tower Museum** at Coward's Bastion, the northwestern corner of the city wall, is its award-winning '**Story of Derry**' exhibition. The museum is open Tuesday–Friday 10:00–16:30.

St Columb's Cathedral, close to Church Bastion, inside the southeast corner of the walls, has **stained-glass windows** showing a number of scenes from the struggle of 1688–89 and there is an audiovisual presentation on **Derry's history**. Open in summer, Monday–Saturday 09:00–17:00; in winter, Monday–Saturday 09:00–13:00, 14:00–16:00.

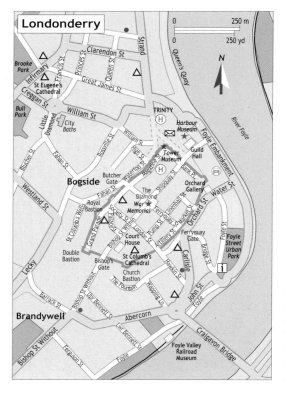

Ulster American Folk Park ★★

At Castletown, some 5km (3 miles) from Omagh city centre on the A5 highway, this **outdoor museum** is dedicated to the thousands of people who emigrated to America in the 18th and 19th centuries – among them the parents of three **US presidents**. It is open April–September, Monday–Saturday 10:30–18:00, Sundays and public holidays 11:00–17:00.

Ulster History Park ★★

At Cullion Village, on the B48 road, this purpose-built attraction traces the **history of Ireland** from the first Stone-Age settlers in around 8000BC to the Protestant Plantation of the 18th century. It is open April–September, Monday–

Saturday 10:30–18:30, Sunday 11:30–19:00, public holidays 10:30–19:00; October–March, Monday– Friday 10:30–17:00.

County Fermanagh

Northern Ireland's westernmost county stretches almost to the Atlantic and is dominated by the indented shorelines and islands of **Lower** and

Above: *Looking east from Lough Macnean Upper, in County Fermanagh.*

Upper Lough Erne, which stretch for more than 70km (43 miles) and cover almost one third of the county. The **Ballinamore-Ballyconnell Canal**, built during the 18th century, connects the Erne and Shannon waterways. The Fermanagh **lakelands** are famous among keen anglers for prize catches of roach, perch, bream, rudd and huge pike.

Enniskillen ★★

Enniskillen, Fermanagh's county town, is situated at the southeastern end of Lower Lough Erne, close to the mouth of the River Erne which connects the two loughs. The ancient stronghold of the **Maguire chieftains**, on the banks of the Erne, now the **Enniskillen Castle Barracks**, contains the regimental museum of the **Royal Inniskilling Fusiliers** (the local regiment) and also the **Fermanagh County Museum**, with displays of regimental banners, weapons, uniforms and an audiovisual presentation. Open May–June and September, Monday and Saturday 14:00–19:00, Tuesday–Friday 10:00–17:00; July–August, Saturday–Monday 14:00–19:00, Tuesday–Friday 10:00–17:00.

Castle Coole, built between 1788 and 1798, is a magnificent **neo-Classical mansion** with a splendid interior which stands on the A4, 2km (1 mile) from the town centre, amid 283ha (700 acres) of **parkland**. Open March–May and September, Saturday–Sunday 12:00–18:00; June–August, daily 12:00–18:00; October Saturday–Sunday 13:00–17:00.

THE O'NEILLS

The O'Neill clan of **Tyrone** were among the most determined opponents of English power in Ireland in the 16th and 17th centuries. **Shane O'Neill** (1530–67), second Earl of Tyrone, took up arms against **Elizabeth I** in 1560, invading the Pale and burning the English settlement at **Armagh** before being defeated by **High Dubh O'Donnell** at **Lough Swilly** in 1567. The **MacDonnell** clan, with whom he sought refuge, killed him and sent his head to Elizabeth's governor, **Lord Deputy Sidney**. His kinsman, **Hugh O'Neill** (1540–1616) first served the English, then in 1598 led the last great revolt of the Gaelic nobles and clans. With the help of Spanish troops landing at **Kinsale**, he nearly succeeded, but was defeated in battle. He submitted, and was pardoned.

Crom Estate ★★★

This reserve comprises some 809ha (2000 acres) of woodland, lakeshore and wetlands beside **Upper Lough Erne**, 5km (3 miles) southwest of Newtownbutler Village. It shelters many rare plant, bird and mammal species. **Boats** can be hired, and there is a night hide for bird and wildlife watchers. Open May–September, daily 10:00–18:00; October–April, Saturday–Sunday 10:00–18:00.

Florence Court ★★

A fine **18th-century mansion** built for the Earls of Enniskillen, with fine Rococo plasterwork. The house stands about 13km (8 miles) southwest of Enniskillen on the A32 road. Open March–May and September, Saturday–Sunday 12:00–18:00; June–August, daily 12:00–18:00.

Belleek

This small village on the Irish border has been famous since the 19th century for its intricate and unique porcelain. At **Belleek Pottery Visitors' Centre** you can watch craftsmen create the elaborate 'basket-woven' porcelain for which Belleek is famous. There is a museum, showroom and shop. Open Monday–Friday 09:00–17:30.

A TASTE OF ULSTER

A Taste of Ulster is a voluntary listings scheme for eating places – including **pubs** and **coffee shops** as well as **restaurants** – guaranteed to offer a sample of traditional and modern dishes created from the region's finest local ingredients. Look out for the distinctive **hexagonal plaque** – many Taste of Ulster members have been singled out by leading food guides.

COUNTY ARMAGH

Armagh is **farming country**, with hills and hedgerows along narrow lanes, bordering County Monaghan in the Republic. On its northern border is **Lough Neagh**, one of Ireland's largest lakes. The visitor attractions of this county are concentrated in and close to the main city, Armagh.

Armagh ★★

Many of Armagh's public buildings were designed by **Francis Johnston**, the local man who was responsible for much of Georgian Dublin. Built in local stone, Armagh is one of the prettiest towns in Northern Ireland.

It is the seat of both the Roman Catholic and Protestant Church of Ireland archbishops of Ireland, and has been **Ireland's spiritual capital** since St Patrick built his first church on the site of the modern Anglican cathedral.

The shell of **St Patrick's (Anglican) Cathedral**, completed in 1842, surrounds an older interior with 18th-century statues and a 13th-century crypt, all that remains of the original medieval cathedral. A plaque marks the grave of **Brian Boru**, High King of Ireland (see page 13).

The **Palace Stables Heritage Centre**, in the stables of the original Archbishop's Palace, portrays a typical day 200 years ago. Open April–September, Monday–Saturday 10:00–18:00, Sunday 13:00–18:00; October–March, Monday–Saturday 10:00–17:00, Sunday 14:00–17:00.

Armagh County Museum ★★

The local museum with art gallery at Mall East contains paintings by the Lurgan-born landscape painter **George Russell** (1867–1935) and Armagh-born portraitist **James Sleator** (1889–1950). Open Monday–Friday 10:00–17:00, Saturday 10:00–13:00, 14:00–17:00.

Navan Centre ★★

About 3km (2 miles) west of the city centre, a vast earthen mound marks the site of **Navan Fort** (Emain Macha), seat of the ancient kings of Ulster.

The interpretative centre at 81 Killylea Road features the **archaeology** and **myths** surrounding Navan. Open Jun–Aug, Mon–Sat 10:00–17:00, Sun 12:00–17:00; Apr–May and Sep, Sat–Sun 10:00–17:00.

TRACE YOUR ULSTER ANCESTORS

If your roots are in Northern Ireland, several organizations in Belfast are able to help you trace your family tree. **The Public Record Office of Northern Ireland (PRONI)**, Balmoral Avenue, Belfast, tel: (01232) 255-905/6, e-mail: proni@doeni.gov.uk has a unique collection of genealogical documents dating back four centuries; the **Ulster Historical Foundation**, 12 College Square East, Belfast, tel: (01232) 332-288, is another useful source of information.

Opposite: *As more Irish people migrate to the cities, bucolic scenes like this are increasingly rare.*

Northern Ireland

Lough Neagh Discovery Centre ★★

On **Oxford Island**, in the centre of the huge expanse of water that dominates the central part of Northern Ireland, the discovery centre features **local history**, with guided walks, bird-watching and boat trips on and around the lough. Open Mon–Fri 09:00–17:00, Sat–Sun 10:00–17:00.

COUNTY DOWN

County Down's 322km (200 miles) of **Irish Sea coastline** are within minutes of Belfast. Hills, moors, beach resorts, medieval churches and Norman castles are among its main attractions. County Down is bounded by two deep inlets – **Belfast Lough** in the north and **Carlingford Lough** in the south. On its east coast, the **Ards Peninsula** is separated from the mainland by **Strangford Lough**, connected to the sea by a narrow channel between Portaferry and Strangford. In the south, the **Mountains of Mourne**, celebrated in song, stretch down to the sea. On the border with the republic, the town of **Newry** has little to lure the visitor other than as a stop en route between Dublin and Belfast.

Bangor

Only 16km (10 miles) east of Belfast, on the coast, Bangor faces out into Belfast Lough and the Irish Sea and is a popular getaway for Belfast people. **Bangor Abbey**, one of the most important abbeys in Ireland, was founded by St Comgall in AD558, and was an important missionary centre for the re-establishment of Christianity in Europe.

Ards Peninsula and Strangford Lough

The Ards Peninsula stretches 32km (20 miles) from the Bangor coast to the southern end of Strangford Lough, and separates Strangford Lough from the Irish Sea. Small **fishing villages** – Donaghadee, Millisle, Ballywalter, Ballyhalbert, Portavogie, Cloughey and Kearney – are dotted along the peninsula's sea coast. The town of Newtownards stands near the north end of the lough.

Scrabo Tower ★★

This Scottish Baronial-style folly with its parapets and battlements was built as a memorial to **Charles William Stewart** (1778–1854), third Marquis of Londonderry. Visitors can climb **122 steps** to the top of the tower for a fine view of Strangford Lough. Signposted from Newtownards town centre, it is open April–September, Saturday–Thursday 10:30–18:00, closed Friday.

Somme Heritage Centre ★★

The focus of this heritage centre at 233 Bangor Road, Newtownards is on the Irish role in **World War I** and at the **Battle of the Somme** in 1916, with an **audiovisual show** and reconstructed model of a trench system. Open October–March, Monday–Thursday 10:00–14:00, Saturday 12:00–16:00; April–June and September, Monday–Thursday 10:00–16:00, Saturday–Sunday 12:00–16:00; July–August, Mon–Friday 10:00–17:00, Saturday–Sunday 12:00–17:00.

Ballycopeland Windmill, Millisle ★

The last working windmill in Ireland, this mill made oatmeal and animal feed until 1915 and is now a **visitors' centre** with interactive displays. It is open Tuesday–Saturday 10:00–18:00, Sunday 14:00–18:00 (year-round).

Mount Stewart House and Gardens ★★

Overlooking Strangford Lough, the **gardens** of Mount Stewart, a superb 18th-century manor house, are among the finest in Europe. The house was the home of the Stewart marquises of Londonderry. Other highlights of the house and gardens include the animal statuary of the **Dodo Terrace**, and also a fine neoclassical folly,

Above: *Sketrick Island, on the east coast.*
Opposite: *Armagh Cathedral, on the site of a medieval building.*

FIONN MACCUMHAILL

The legendary warrior Fionn MacCumhaill (or **Finn Mac-Cool**) acquired his wisdom after catching and eating the divine Salmon of Knowledge, **Fintan**. The High King **Cormac MacArt** later made him captain of his bodyguard, the **Fianna**, and he went on to many fantastic adventures, battling gods, monsters and other heroes. Finn, like the British **King Arthur**, is a semi-mythical character. According to legend, he and his warriors lived during the latter half of the 3rd century AD, and King Cormac ruled from AD254–277. Like Arthur and his knights, Finn and the Fianna are said to be sleeping in a cavern until Ireland again has need for them.

Above: *Lush landscapes at Dundrum, looking out to the Mountains of Mourne.*

known as the **Temple of the Winds**, built in 1785 by James 'Athenian' Stuart.

Greyabbey ★★

Much ruined but still fascinating, the remains of a 12th-century Cistercian abbey are located just outside Greyabbey Village on the A20 Portaferry Road. The grounds are beautifully maintained and there is an interesting medieval **Physic Garden**. Currently closed for renovations.

Downpatrick

Downpatrick, in the heart of the county, is graced by the attractive Victorian Gothic **Down Cathedral**, rebuilt in the 19th century, which stands on the site of an earlier 14th-century building. **St Patrick** is said to be buried in its churchyard. Open usual church hours.

Castle Ward House and Gardens ★★

At Strangford Village on the A20, Castle Ward is a fine, **two-fronted manor house** built in 1862 for Bernard Ward, Lord Bangor, and his wife Lady Anne Darnley. The garden front, facing the lough, is in the Gothic style favoured by Lady Anne, while the entrance front, facing the driveway, is in the Palladian style chosen by her husband. Open April–September, daily 10:00–20:00; October–March, daily 10:00–16:00.

Silent Valley Forest Park and Reservoir

This spectacular **man-made lake** in the midst of the Mountains of Mourne is surrounded by some of Northern Ireland's most striking landscapes. It is open daily May–September 10:00–18:30; October–April 10:00–16:00.

Northern Ireland at a Glance

By Air: Flights from UK mainland and European airports to Belfast Airport, tel: (02890) 457-745, and Derry Airport, tel: (02871) 810-784.
By Sea: Ferries to Belfast from Liverpool, Isle of Man, Stranraer and Campbeltown; to Larne from Cairnryan in Scotland.
By Rail: From Dublin via Newry by Northern Ireland Railways, Central Station, East Bridge Street, Belfast, tel: (02890) 899-400, and by Irish Rail, 35 Lower Abbey Street, Dublin, tel: (01) 703-4669.

By Bus: Ulsterbus, tel: (02890) 333-000, operates bus services from Belfast throughout Northern Ireland.
By Train: Rail services are operated by Northern Ireland Railways (*see* above). Trains depart from Belfast to Londonderry, via Antrim, Ballymena and Coleraine.

Belfast
LUXURY
Europa Hotel, Great Victoria Street, Belfast, tel: (02890) 271-066, fax: (02890) 266-099. Belfast's top four-star hotel, with health centre, pool and business centre.
Wellington Park Hotel, 21 Mallone Road, Belfast, tel: (02890) 381-111, fax: (02890) 665-410. An institute in Belfast for its comfort, style and family-run atmosphere.

MID-RANGE
Park Avenue Hotel, 158 Holywood Road, Belfast, tel: (02890) 656-520, fax: (02890) 471-417. Comfortable two-star hotel with 70 rooms.

Derry
LUXURY
Radisson Roe Park Hotel and Golf Resort, Limavady, Londonderry, tel: (02877) 722-222, fax: (02877) 722-313. Lavish golf resort and country club, with own 18-hole course, fine views, health club and spa.

MID-RANGE
Beech Hill Country House Hotel, 32 Ardmore Road, Londonderry, tel: (02871) 349-279, fax: (02871) 345-366. Comfortable three-star hotel.

Belfast
LUXURY
Nick's Warehouse, 35 Hill Street, tel: (02890) 439-690. Highly commendable restaurant and wine bar, specialities include duck with apple and halibut with langoustine.
Restaurant 44, 44 Bedford Street, tel: (02890) 244-844. Casserole of shellfish and char-grilled fillet of beef among the recommendations.

MID-RANGE
O'Neill's, 4 Joy's Entry, tel: (02890) 326-711, fax: (02890) 329-869. Good food, wine list, live music at weekends.
Speranza, 16 Shaftesbury Square, tel: (02890) 230-213. Good value Italian restaurant, pizza and pasta.

Londonderry
LUXURY
Beech Hill Country House Hotel, 32 Ardmore Road, tel: (02871) 349-279. Good restaurant in Derry's best hotel.

MID-RANGE
Brown's Bar and Brasserie, 1 Bonds Hill, tel: (02871) 345-180. Modern European dishes including seafood, vegetarian meals and Irish lamb.

Bailey's Historical Pub Tours of Belfast, April–September, depart Tuesdays 19:00 and Saturdays 16:00 from Flannigan's, Great Victoria Street, tel: (02890) 246-609, fax: (01247) 882-596.
Citybus Tours, tel: (02890) 626-888, runs coach tours of Belfast departing Wednesday, Thursday, Saturday and Sunday at 13:00 from Castle Place.

Tourism Development Office, Belfast City Council, Cecil Ward Building, 4–10 Linenhall Street, Belfast BT2 8BP, tel: (02890) 320-202 ext 3585.
Derry Tourist Information Centre, 44 Foyle Street, Derry, tel: (02871) 369-501.
Armagh Tourist Information Centre, 40 English Street, Armagh, tel: (02837) 521-800.

Travel Tips

Tourist Information

The **Irish Tourist Board** (*Bord Failte*) has offices in Frankfurt, London, New York, Sydney, Auckland and Johannesburg, as well as in Belfast and Londonderry. Head office and information centre is at Baggot Street Bridge, Dublin 2, tel: (01) 602-4000, fax: (01) 602-4100. Address for postal enquiries is PO Box 273, Dublin 8. Bord Failte's Internet site is: www.ireland.ie
Bord Failte's computerized reservation and information system, called **Gulliver**, at all main tourist information offices gives up-to-date information on events and attractions in Ireland. You can also use Gulliver to book accommodation and sightseeing tours.

The **Northern Ireland Tourist Board** has offices in London, Dublin, Glasgow, Frankfurt, New York and Toronto. Head office is at 59 North Street, Belfast BT1 1NB, tel: (02890) 231-221, fax: (02890) 240-960. Information on Northern Ireland is available from **British Tourist Authority** offices in Chicago, Auckland, Hong Kong, Singapore and Johannesburg.

Embassies and Consulates:
Republic of Ireland
Australia: 6th floor, Fitzwilton House, Wilton Terrace, Dublin 2, tel: (01) 664-5300.
Canada: 4th floor, 65–68 St Stephen's Green, Dublin 2, tel: (01) 417-4100.
UK: 29 Merrion Road, Dublin 4, tel: (01) 205-3700.
USA: 42 Elgin Road, Dublin 4, tel: (01) 668-8777.
Northern Ireland
Diplomatic and consular affairs for Northern Ireland are handled by relevant embassies in London.
Australia: Australian High Commission, Australia House, Strand, London WC8, tel: (0171) 379-4334.
Canada: Canadian High Commission, Canada House, 5 Trafalgar Square, London WC2, tel: (0171) 258-6600.
New Zealand: New Zealand High Commission, New Zealand House, Haymarket, London SW1Y, tel: (0171) 930-8422.
South Africa: South African High Commission, South Africa House, Trafalgar Square, London WC2, tel: (0171) 451-7299.
USA: 24 Grosvenor Square, London W1A, tel: (0171) 499-6000.

Entry Requirements

Citizens of European Union countries, the USA, Canada, Australia, New Zealand, and South Africa do not need **visas** to enter the Republic of Ireland and Northern Ireland for holidays of less than three months.

Customs

Normal European Union customs requirements apply to visitors arriving in Ireland and Northern Ireland. **Duty-free** goods are not available for travel within the European Union from 1999. Under EU guidelines travellers within the EU may bring duty-paid goods including up to 50 litres of beer, 25 litres of wine, and 800 cigarettes. Travellers from non-EU countries may bring in 200 cigarettes, 1 litre of spirits, 2 litres of wine, 50 grams of perfume and 20cc of toilet water.

Health Requirements

There are no special health requirements for visitors to Ireland or Northern Ireland.

Getting There

By Air: Frequent flights to Dublin, Cork and Belfast from most major British cities including all four London airports, Birmingham, Liverpool, Manchester, Glasgow, Edinburgh, Plymouth, Bristol and Exeter. **Aer Lingus**, **Ryanair** and other independent airlines and European carriers also operate between Dublin, Cork, and Belfast and key European cities including Amsterdam, Frankfurt and Paris. There are international flights to Shannon and Knock airports in central Ireland. Aer Lingus and other carriers connect Dublin and Shannon with main gateways in the USA and Canada including New York, Boston and Chicago.

By Sea: Daily ferries to Dublin and Dun Laoghaire from Liverpool and from Holyhead in Wales, to Cork from Swansea and from Roscoff in France, and to Belfast and Larne from Stranraer and Cairnryan in Scotland and from Liverpool.

By Coach: Bus Eireann, Ireland's national bus service, operates coach services via ferries from Dublin, Cork and other major towns to London, Birmingham, Glasgow, Liverpool and other mainland British points. CIE International Tours, with offices in London, New York, Paris, Düsseldorf and Dublin, specializes in coach tour packages.

What to Pack

Ireland's unpredictable (and frequently wet) climate means you should pack waterproof outer wear and comfortable wet-weather footwear whenever you go. A hat or umbrella may be welcome in summer and essential in winter. Be prepared for colder weather from September to May. A sweater will be useful all year. Dress codes in restaurants, night spots and hotels are relaxed. Smart-casual wear is acceptable for most occasions. All medicines and travel accessories from batteries to band-aids are available throughout Ireland so there is no need to bring these from home.

Money Matters

Currency: In 2002 the Republic of Ireland adopted the euro as its official currency. Notes are available in 5, 10, 20, 50, 100, 200 and 500 euro denominations, with coins of 1 euro, 2 euros, 50 cents, 20 cents, 10 cents, 5 cents, 2 cents and 1 cent.

Northern Ireland's currency is the pound sterling, in common with the rest of the UK. The pound is divided into 100 pence in denominations of 1p, 2p, 5p, 10p, 20p and 50p. £1 and new £2 coins are also in circulation with notes of £5, £10, £20, £50 and £100. Northern Ireland has its own currency notes which are in theory legal tender throughout the UK, but English retailers may refuse them. They are also difficult to exchange outside the UK and Ireland, so if travelling on to Europe, convert any leftover Northern Ireland notes into Bank of England sterling notes.

Changing money: Banks in Northern Ireland are open Monday–Friday 09:30–16:30 (may close 12:30–13:30 in smaller towns). Banks in the Republic of Ireland are open Monday–Friday 10:00–16:00, and until 17:00 on Thursdays. Numerous *bureaux de change* in the main cities offer foreign currency services outside normal banking hours.

Credit cards: All major credit

USEFUL PHRASES

You don't need to speak Irish to visit Ireland – indeed, in most of the country trying to do so will be greeted with incomprehension. However, if you are visiting one of the few Gaeltacht areas (in parts of Kerry, Galway, Mayo and Donegal) where the language is still in everyday use along with English, you may want to try a few simple phrases:

Hello • *Dia dhuit*
Goodbye • *Slan agat*
Welcome • *Failte*
Cheers • *Slainte*
Please • *Le do thoil*
Thank you • *Go raibh maith aguth*

In addition, signs in the Republic of Ireland may be in both English and Irish. These include:

Toilet • *Leithreas*
Men • *Fir*
Women • *Mna*
Police • *Gardai*
Post office • *Oifig an Phoist*

Be aware that in Northern Ireland, use of the Irish language has strong political connotations, implying strong nationalist sympathies.

cards are accepted in larger stores, hotels and restaurants, but smaller establishments may prefer payment in cash. All bank cash machines accept international Visa, Access, Mastercard, Cirrus Plus and Maestro cards.

Tipping: A 10 per cent tip will be welcomed by hotel porters, taxi drivers and table staff in restaurants and cafés, but tipping is not usual in bars and pubs.

Tax: Visitors from outside the European Union may reclaim Value Added Tax (VAT) on purchases (but not on services) through the Cashback scheme in the Republic of Ireland (look for the Cashback logo on shop fronts) and on departure from the UK. VAT reclaim forms are available on arrival in the UK.

Accommodation

Ireland and Northern Ireland have a wide range of accommodation to suit all budgets and tastes. Beyond Dublin, large international chain **hotels** are thin on the ground and outnumbered by individual, locally owned and managed hotels, many offering high levels of comfort and luxury. Outside main cities, even in small towns, addresses often do not include street numbers as country houses, pubs and hotels are often regarded as landmarks in their own right. Ask for precise local directions when making your reservation. The Irish Tourist Board, with the Irish Hotel Federation, operates a two-tier classification system for hotels and guesthouses, rating them from one to five stars. A similar system is operated by the Northern Ireland Tourist Board. **Guesthouses** are not required to offer as wide a range of services and facilities as full-service hotels, but guesthouse accommodation is not inferior, and many guesthouses offer standards well above the requirements for their category. Quality control by Bord Failte and the NITB is strict, and many visitors find family-run guesthouses offer excellent value for money and an even warmer personal welcome than the larger hotels. Other options include luxurious mansions and country houses, fishing lodges, farmhouse rooms on working farms, camping (recommended only in summer) and caravanning in rural areas. More novel alternatives include traditional horse-drawn caravans and river cruisers on the Shannon Waterway.

Eating Out

Most restaurants in the Republic of Ireland are subject to high-rate VAT at 21 per cent, so eating out can be expensive, especially with wine, as the price of even an undistinguished bottle of plonk can be alarmingly high. Prices in Northern Ireland are somewhat lower, thanks to a lower rate of tax. Few other Irish cities can match the range of eating places in Dublin, where restaurants range from grand old establishments to European-style cafés. In both Northern Ireland and the Republic, pubs offer a wide choice of good plain cooking, with Ireland noted for its seafood and its fine beef.

Transport

Air: Within Ireland, distances are short and there is little point in air travel. However, there are air connections between Dublin and Belfast, and from both these cities to Cork, Ireland's second city.

Rail: Iarnrod Eireann (Irish Rail) operates routes to main cities from Dublin, with direct intercity services between Dublin and Cork, Limerick, Galway and other major cities. An international express route (eight services daily) connects

CONVERSION CHART

From	To	Multiply By
Millimetres	Inches	0.0394
Metres	Yards	1.0936
Metres	Feet	3.281
Kilometres	Miles	0.6214
Square kilometres	Square miles	0.386
Hectares	Acres	2.471
Litres	Pints	1.760
Kilograms	Pounds	2.205
Tonnes	Tons	0.984

To convert Celsius to Fahrenheit: $x \; 9 \div 5 + 32$

Dublin with Belfast. In Northern Ireland, main rail routes connect Belfast with Londonderry, Larne and Bangor.
Bus: Bus Eireann has inter-city and rural bus routes throughout the Republic of Ireland. In Northern Ireland, express coaches run between Belfast and all main towns. An express bus service operates between Dublin and Belfast seven times a day, taking three hours. Bus Eireann offers various tickets covering a range of regions and time periods. More details are available at www.bus eireann.ie
Car: Car rental is available at all airports and downtown offices in Dublin, Belfast and major cities. Drive on the left in both Ireland and Northern Ireland. In the Republic of Ireland, road signs are in both Irish and English. In Northern Ireland, be prepared to stop for Royal Ulster Constabulary or British Army checkpoints. Many hotels and guesthouses offer free off-street parking (recommended in Dublin where theft of and from vehicles is common). EU driving licences are valid, but non-EU visitors may need an International Driving Licence, obtainable on arrival through motoring organizations or before you leave home. Speed limits unless otherwise indicated are 50kph (30mph) in towns and 115kph (70mph) on highways. Full collision damage waiver (CDW) and liability insurance is recommended when renting. Drivers and passengers must wear seatbelts. If using your own vehicle you will need

registration documents, proof of valid insurance, driving licence or international permit. In the Republic of Ireland, your car may not be driven by an Irish resident during your stay, except a garage employee with your written permission. Six highways radiate from Dublin, linking it with the rest of Ireland. Anticlockwise, these are the N1 coastal highway north to Drogheda and on into Northern Ireland, (where it becomes the A1 Belfast highway); the N2 and N3, northwest to Meath and beyond; the N4 and N7, respectively west and southwest through Kildare; and the N11 coastal highway south through Wicklow. In Northern Ireland, the A1 runs from Newry to Belfast, the A2 coastal highway from Larne in the north through Belfast to link with the A1 at Newry, and the A5 connects Belfast with Londonderry and the northwest.

Business Hours

Banks open Monday–Friday 10:00–16:00 and until 17:00 on Thursdays in the Republic of Ireland, 09:30–16:30 in Northern Ireland. Most shops and offices open 09:00–17:30. In Dublin, shops are open until 20:00 on Thursdays. Elsewhere shops close at midday on Wednesday and Saturday in many smaller towns and villages. A few supermarkets in larger towns open Sunday 12:00–18:00.

Time Difference

Ireland and Northern Ireland use GMT in winter and GMT +1 in summer.

Communications

The area dialling code for Dublin is (01) for calls within the Republic of Ireland and (11850) for calls from abroad. To call the operator, dial 114; directory enquiries, tel: 11850; international calls may be made from any public phone through the operator.
The area dialling code for Belfast is (02890) for calls within the UK and (00 44 2890) for calls from abroad and Northern Ireland directory enquiries is 118500. To call the operator, dial 100; directory enquiries, tel: 192; international calls from any phone.

Electricity

Standard supply is 230V in Ireland (3-pin flat sockets or 2-pin round wall sockets), 240V (3-pin flat sockets only) in Northern Ireland.

Weights and Measures

Measurements in Ireland and UK are officially metric but many people still think in terms of miles, not kilometres, pounds and ounces rather than grams and kilograms, and pints and quarts rather than litres.

Health Precautions

No special precautions need be

taken when travelling in Ireland and Northern Ireland.

Health Services

European Union residents holding a European Health Insurance Card (EHIC), available from your doctor or health department before leaving, are entitled to free medical and hospital treatment.

Safety and Security

Both Ireland and Northern Ireland have low rates of theft and violence, especially away from big cities. Violent crime against visitors is very rare, as is theft from hotel rooms. However, Dublin has a relatively high crime rate due to youth unemployment and drug addiction rates, and theft from vehicles, pickpocketing and bag snatching are not uncommon. Despite the Troubles of the 1970s–1990s, Northern Ireland (political and sectarian violence aside) has remarkably low levels of crime and from the visitor's point of view is a safe destination. Few if any visitors have been killed or injured in the violence of the last 30 years. To put things in perspective: more people are killed in car accidents on British roads each year than in the entire 30 years of the Troubles.

Emergencies

Ireland and Northern Ireland: police, fire, ambulance and lifeboat service, tel: **999**.

Language

Irish is the official language of Ireland and is sometimes used by militant Nationalists in

Northern Ireland as a badge of national sentiment. However, more than a century of efforts to revive Irish as the national language have failed to supplant English as first language of Ireland. Attempts to communicate in Irish are more than likely to be met with baffled incomprehension or laughter!

Road Signs

Road signs are standard European signage, symbols and numerals and are immediately easy to decipher even if you are not familiar with them. Street names are in English.

Best Buys

High-quality souvenirs offered in specialty shops include glass and crystal, silver, woollen knitwear, Irish linen and Irish tweed, fine porcelain and pewter. Irish whiskey is another good buy. The Guinness Brewery in Dublin sells an assortment of Guinness-related clothing and memorabilia. Irish markets and shops can be a happy hunting ground for antique buyers: look out for Georgian, Victorian and Edwardian silverware, clocks and watches, jewellery and antiquarian books and prints.

GOOD READING

Colin Bateman, *Of Wee Sweetie Mice and Men* (HarperCollins, 0006496121).
Dermot Bolger, *Dublin Quartet* (New Island Books 0140482350).
Colm Toibin, *The Irish Famine* (Profile Books 1861971443).
Christy Browne, *My Left Foot* (Minerva 0749391774).
Tim Pat Coogan, *Michael Collins* (Arrow 0099685809).
J P Donleavy, *The Ginger Man* (Abacus, 0349108501).
Roddy Doyle, *The Snapper* (0749391251), *The Commitments* (0749391685), *The Van* (0749399902), *Paddy Clarke Ha Ha Ha* (0749397357) and *The Woman Who Walked into Walls* (0749395990), all in Minerva.
Bill Flanagan, *U2: At the End of the World* (Bantam 0553408062).
Thomas Flanagan, *The End of The Hunt* (Mandarin 0749319836).
Bob Geldof, *Is That It?* (Penguin 014009363X). Autobiography by the rock star and campaigner.
Oliver St John Gogarty, *As I Was Going Down Sackville Street* (O'Brien Press 0862783941).
Seamus Heaney, *Seeing Things* (Faber 0571144691) and *New Selected Poems* (Faber 0571143725).
James Joyce, *Dubliners* (Wordsworth 1853260487).
Patrick Kavanagh, *Selected Poems* (Penguin 0140184856).
Pat Liddy, *Walking Dublin* (New Holland 1 85368 485 6)
Flann O'Brien (Brian O'Nolan), *At-Swim-Two-Birds* (Penguin 0140181725), *The Best of Myles* (HarperCollins 0586089500), *The Third Policeman* (HarperCollins 0586087494) and *The Dalkey Archive* (HarperCollins 0586089500).
David Sharrock and Mark Davenport, *Man of War, Man of Peace: The Unauthorised Biography of Gerry Adams* (Pan 1997).

INDEX

Note: Numbers in **bold**
indicate photographs